SACRED
EARTH

SACRED EARTH

THE SPIRITUAL LANDSCAPE OF NATIVE AMERICA

ARTHUR VERSLUIS

INNER TRADITIONS INTERNATIONAL
ROCHESTER, VERMONT

Inner Traditions International, Ltd.
One Park Street
Rochester, Vermont 05767

Library of Congress Cataloging-in-Publication Data

Versluis, Arthur, 1959-
    Sacred earth: the spiritual landscape of native America / Arthur Versluis.
          p.   cm.
    Includes bibliographical references and index.
    ISBN 0-89281-352-0
    1. Indians of North America—Religion and mythology. 2. Human ecology—Religious aspects. 3. Nature—Religious aspects.
    4. Sacred space. I. Title.
E98.R3V47 1991
299'.7—dc20   91-30090
                                                CIP

Printed and bound in the United States

10 9 8 7 6 5 4 3

Distributed to the book trade in Canada by Publishers Group West (PGW), Toronto, Ontario
Distributed to the book trade in the United Kingdom by Deep Books, London
Distributed to the book trade in Australia by Millennium Books, Newtown, N.S.W.
Distributed to the book trade in New Zealand by Tandem Press, Auckland

This great drama might be defined as the struggle . . . between urban civilization (in the strictly human and pejorative sense of this term, with all its implications of artifice and servility) and the kingdom of Nature considered as the majestic, pure, limitless raiment of the Divine Spirit. And it is from the idea of the final victory of Nature (final because it is primordial) that the Indians draw their inexhaustible patience in the fact of the misfortunes of their race; Nature, of which they feel themselves to be embodiments, and which is at the same time their sanctuary, will end by conquering this artificial and sacrilegious world, for it is the Garment, the Breath, the very Hand of the Great Spirit.

—*Frithjof Schuon,* The Feathered Sun

CONTENTS

INTRODUCTION

This book was written to reveal not entertainment from the past, not the equivalent of museum displays unconnected to our actual lives, but a way of understanding the human place in this world. It was written that we might together come to understand how the original people in the Americas live— sacred people on a sacred earth. But insofar as the spiritual truths and practices of the Native American spiritual traditions reflect the universal inheritance of humanity, what we discuss here is intended not just for Americans, but for all peoples. The hour is late for spiritual reawakening, but it is still possible. This book was written to help bring the traditional understanding of the human place on this earth into general understanding again before it is too late.

We all feel a longing for something we cannot name, and we feel that longing more intensely the further we divorce ourselves from nature and from religious tradition. Often we seek to satisfy this longing through acquisition, through attaining power, or through other people, but somehow externals never really fill that emptiness within us; we remain restless and dissatisfied, always looking for something or someone else. This is a condition peculiarly intense in the modern era. We know we have lost something precious, but we are not quite certain anymore what it is.

1

Many people today also recognize that ours is a world out of kilter. We hear talk of the "ecological crisis," and we can see its results all around us, in barren lands and eroded hills, dry riverbeds and oil-soaked shorelines, in radioactive deserts, in poisoned winds and waters. Of course, the environmental movement opposes this destruction of trees and animals and waters and air and earth. But it substitutes for human destructiveness merely a rational management program. Even corporations and conglomerates use "ecological marketing" as a device to sell more products.

Environmentalism divorced from a spiritual understanding of the human place in the cosmos is simply a sublimated version of the very mentality that is causing the destruction. Environmentalists, as much as the exploiters they oppose, largely view things from a positivist or materialist perspective and consequently are unable to do more than organize against this or that manifestation of modern civilization's destructiveness. This is not enough. One can temporarily, on the basis of rational argument or physical intervention, stop destruction of a particular forest, perhaps, but the same forces will in the meantime destroy two forests somewhere else.

Modern civilization is inherently omnivorous. It eats everything around it; it lays waste to everything it touches. To put it more accurately, we as individuals lay waste to everything we touch. Because we are out of balance, so is our world. Look at our cities: everywhere they become more desolate, places of ever-intensifying violence; everywhere the countryside is devastated, paved over and mined, dug up and built over, left as sterile as if it had been laid waste by an invading army, but that army is we ourselves. We salt the earth where we live. We are each a part of that destruction; we cannot blame it on someone else. It is you and I who do this, and we alone who must change things.

We cannot cease destroying, and we will not fill that emptiness within, until we effect a spiritual renaissance. Only when we—each of us individually—turn toward spiritual truth, and open ourselves to that truth, will we strike at the heart of that imbalance we see all around us in this world. The key to regenerating our world lies in realizing the spiritual reality of which our world is a reflection. Only when we open ourselves to the transcendent reality with which humanity has always lived can we begin to change our approach to the world around us. We cannot fix our world or satisfy our nameless longing with technology; we must ourselves be regenerated.

There are dangers in this path of spiritual renaissance. Some today advocate "modern shamanism," as though we could simply jettison our modern lives and become shamans for an evening, as though a spiritual path were an entertainment, rather like cinema, only with better special effects. Nothing could be further from the truth. Certain books, for instance, make autochthonous American spirituality nothing more than entertainment full of "magical," drug-induced, or bizarre events. Whatever their authors' intentions, the result of these books has been to inject into the popular consciousness bizarre images of Native American spirituality, and to lure some people into various aberrant forms of what they believe to be some kind of modern shamanism.

Conditioned by forces of which we are for the most part scarcely aware, but knowing that we lack something, many of us seek wonderful, miraculous, entertaining events. Levitations, possessions, all manner of supernatural things attract us. After several centuries of materialism—which has become like a carapace cutting us off from the Divine—many of us have forgotten what spirituality is, have forgotten the contentment and serenity that it brings. Consequently, we look for "signs." But we forget that there is such a thing as evil. We forget that there are those who masquerade as spiritual teachers, but who have no tradition, who lead their followers into the pit.

Authentic religious tradition protects us from such evil and guides us toward truth. But how do we, whose whole conditioning has been to reject the past and to look toward the future, how can we connect again with tradition? What can we do, now, to regenerate our understanding of the world, to accept anew the age-old task of humanity—to become human? Even in antiquity, when people's lives were immersed in their religious traditions, it was said that the spiritual path is like a razor's edge, difficult to walk. How might we today be able to follow such a path, when we have so little support and so many obstacles?

That is the crux of our dilemma. But what was true in antiquity is true today, and shall always be true, so long as there are people on Earth. The spiritual path is open to us today and must always be open to us. Just because the outward spiritual supports that existed in traditional societies are to a large extent not available for us does not mean we ought to despair. Ours is a destructive age, to be sure, but it is also a time when, as a compensation, knowledge of all the world's religious traditions is available to us, a time when the passing of all things is forced upon us, a time when the essential becomes clearer by contrast to the inessential things surrounding us and clamoring for our attention. That which causes our sorrow is also a gift.

In such an era, the autochthonous religious traditions like the Australian Aboriginal and the Native American take on a special significance for all peoples. Modern civilization continues to separate itself from the natural world by countless means. Most people live in air-conditioned isolation, almost wholly separated from the cycles of heat and cold, rain and snow; for most people today, not only the spirit-beings of the natural world but the natural world itself is foreign, unknown, except as filtered through "entertainment." Even farmland is endangered; we use land up as if it were a commodity. But though we know that our civilization is destroying us and our world, we don't see the alternative. Here the spirituality of the original peoples is essential.

Such spirituality speaks to us not just of avoiding dumping deadly toxins into rivers and streams, not just of ceasing to bulldoze sacred lands and stopping the destruction of what forest and open land we have left, but of our spiritual relationship to the natural world. It speaks to the very heart of how we live. Many contemporary observers have suggested that from original peoples we can learn how better to balance our impact on the natural world, as though traditional spirituality amounted to nothing more than avoiding our customary destructiveness, recognizing where there are watersheds and game and natural balances. But spirituality is much more than that.

In this book we will write—to the limited degree that this is possible— of the great mystery that is at the heart of human life on this earth and of how we can live in the way that we were meant to live. This is a book intended to bring into general consciousness an awareness of the spirituality of the landscape and beings surrounding us. Human beings are not isolated, mechanical creatures who live in warrens, who are programmed by "mass media," who consume, who sleep, and who die. We are spiritual beings in a spiritual cosmos. The heritage preserved by the original peoples reveals to us our own primordial inheritance as spiritual beings, whatever our backgrounds.

Each of us must come to terms with our place in this world as spiritual beings. To do so is to enter into the unutterable richness of a deeper understanding; to refuse is to close oneself off from our spiritual inheritance and from the spiritual significance of our life on earth. Whatever one's tradition, be it Christian, Jewish, Buddhist, Muslim, or one of the other world religions, it is essential to come to terms with one's place on this earth. To do this, it is important to turn to the indigenous peoples, especially in America, a continent whose history has been one of constant destruction of the original peoples and their deep understanding of the human purpose.

As John Collier wrote in 1947:

> They had what the world has lost. They have it now. . . . What the world has lost, the world must have again, lest it die. Not many years are left to have or have not, to recapture the lost ingredient. . . . They had and have this power for living which our modern world has lost—as world-view and self-view, as tradition and institution, as practical philosophy dominating their societies and as an art supreme among all the arts. . . . True, the deep cause of our world agony is that we have lost that passion and reverence for human personality and for the web of life and the earth which the American Indians have tended as a central, sacred fire since [time immemorial]. Our *long* hope is to renew that sacred fire in us all. It is our only long hope.[1]

The urgency of this call cannot be overlooked. Neither can the essence of our only long hope: to discover anew the spiritual truth without which life on this earth is an empty thing. We must see the Earth around us again the way it was meant to be seen; we must recognize the spiritual meanings of the sky and earth and waters, of the mountains and rivers and rocks. We must again become grounded on this Earth. It is time.

This is a book about a visionary America, an America of the spirit. There is an America whose history and identity are synonymous with mass production, technology, and industrialism. With this we are all too familiar. But in the pages that follow, we offer a different view—a vision of America as primordial, as a spiritual land across its length and breadth. Although we will focus on specific sacred places, chiefly in the Great Plains—and particularly in Kansas—these sites are synechdochic, standing for the whole. For in this book we will consider America as holy place.

PART I
FOUNDATIONS

1
Nature as Theophany

Standing on a bluff, around us the horizon's circle, above heaven's great dome, and in every direction rolling hills fading into the haze of distance: here, in the center of a continent, where springs flow, where the earth rises up beneath us and holds us up against the sky, we feel what it is to be a human being standing on the earth. We feel what it is to be alive, and everywhere is a deep, incommunicable, upwelling gratitude for life. Everywhere around us is spiritual power, the unwritten spiritual truth inscribed on the heavens and in the earth, in the creatures of the air and the earth and the waters. In virgin nature are we grounded, and without her we cannot truly live.

Before the vast, wild, inexpressible, subtle beauty of the virgin wilderness, petty human concerns fall away. Faced with the absolute grandeur of nature in solitude, we cannot but stand in reverence before her. We know this intuitively; it is why the first signs of discontent with modernity focus on the destruction of the natural world. In virgin nature is the living antidote to the poisons created by our virulent civilization, and so in proportion as those poisons grow more toxic and prevalent do human beings turn back toward what is left of the natural world.

Modern civilization is coming to recognize that it is destroying the natural world—but merely to see that this or that species is being obliterated is not enough. Nor is it even enough to observe rationally that we are destroying life in a given place, or on the whole Earth. We have to look more deeply, at *why* this destruction is taking place. From the perspective of the original peoples, we are destroying nature because we are blind to nature as theophany or divine revelation. Humanity has a spiritual relationship to the world, and our world destruction represents a spiritual blindness.[2]

Nothing reveals this spiritual blindness more clearly than the attempted justifications for the depredation of the last remaining wilderness areas on this earth. One finds corporation spokespeople arguing that we have an obligation to our economic system to go forth and extract "natural resources" from wherever they remain. This kind of predatory language reveals a total incomprehension of the Earth's significance. The land is not merely a repository for "natural resources"; it is a living manifestation of the Divine.

Fundamentally, there are two kinds of people in question here. On the one hand is Promethean man, standing over a ruined land, filled with himself and his power over the earth. On the other hand is reverential man, standing in humility and blessed with spiritual power. To Promethean man, the earth and sky and water are merely things to be used for his own aggrandizement; to reverential man, the earth and sky and water and all the creatures bespeak their immortal spiritual Origin. This is why reverential man bows down in reverence before all things; and this is why Promethean man, at heart, fears and consumes all things.

Promethean man has forgotten who he is. Having forgotten his spiritual Origin and significance, he seeks to fill a lack within himself. He wants something, but is not sure what that something is and so seeks everywhere to fill it by consuming the world around him. This is the origin of modern science, of modern technology, of modern consumerism. This is also why the history of modern civilization is the history of ever-greater conflagration: once we forgot our spiritual Origin and our nature as reverential man, we began a headlong movement into ever-greater forgetfulness and ever-greater destruction.

To this time-bound forgetfulness, destruction, and conflagration, virgin nature stands serenely indifferent. In her trees, crags, valleys, bluffs, waters, animals, fish, birds, and other animals, we see anew our place as reverential people, standing between timelessness above and time below. Modern civilization likes to believe that time is all, that the physical world "evolved" to finally produce human life, as though we were the pinnacle of all things, "freed" from nature's bonds at last.[3] But virgin nature reveals the timeless truth at the center of things, and her majesty demonstrates to us how laughable are our theories and notions about her, our absurd calculations.

By "virgin nature" I do not necessarily mean nature wholly free from human influences—for one could well argue that no such places any longer exist on Earth. Rather, "virgin nature" refers to sacred wild places that still maintain their numinosity, or spiritual power. (Although the term has been abused to mean "land ripe for exploitation," misuse does not invalidate its original and noble meaning.) The disserting Supreme Court opinion reproduced in the Appendix discusses precisely such a sacred wild place. Increasingly rare, virgin nature shows us an essential aspect of what it means to be human.

Furthermore, when we speak of nature as theophany, as a manifestation of the Divine, we are, in fact, referring to that great mystery at the heart of all wilderness and of the countless spirits who are its revealers—whose signs and seals are the rock paintings, sandstone carvings, and earth monuments. All nature bodies forth the Divine imprint, and in these carvings or drawings we see not crude "animistic" symbols but the signs of the countless spirits everywhere in the natural world.

We exist in a whirl of images and noises, sounds, lights, desires, frustrations, pleasures, sufferings. Our lives are a cacophony; insulated from wind and rain and sun, from heat and cold, we are ensphered in our own catacombs of metal and concrete and plastic. Living in such a world, is it any wonder that we turn to drugs, to ever more sensational means of stimulation, to entertainment that renders us catatonic? Insulated from nature, ungrounded, why should we be surprised at our own brutality? Where, in such a world, is there room for gratitude, and for what should we be grateful?

Yet gratitude and reverence are the heart of what virgin nature and aboriginal religions have to teach us. We are given everything, not to use up and destroy but to offer back to our spiritual Origin what has been given, to redeem ourselves. Our attitude toward the Divine must be gratitude; our attitude toward what has been given must be reverence. We are to revere the natural world not in an idolatrous way but because nature is everywhere a gift, everywhere a mystery, everywhere divine revelation.

This awareness of nature's true meaning is found among all the world religious traditions. In Zen Buddhism one finds it succinctly put by Bunan Zenji, who said, "Grass, trees, land, country—all these are the Way of the Dharma." And as to our technological achievements, there too traditional religions have something to say. Ummon Zenji, another Zen Buddhist teacher, said, "There is nothing in this world so wonderful but that it may be better not to have it at all." The great Muslim scholar Seyyed Hossain Nasr wrote, "It must never be forgotten that for non–modern man—whether he be ancient or contemporary . . . the cosmos speaks to man, and all of its phenomena contain meaning. They are symbols of a higher degree of reality."[4] Such quotations, from Christian, Jewish, Muslim, Hindu, and Buddhist sources, could be multiplied indefinitely.

For indigenous peoples in particular, however, virgin nature is sacred. Everything in the natural world embodies spiritual truth. Seated on the high bluff, we are not looking at mere matter that "evolved" into its current form. Rather, in the hawk that circles over there, high above the ridge that runs behind us to the south, is manifested spiritual energy. The hawk is not just a creature, divorced from us; it bodies forth the spiritual archetype of which it is at once symbol and manifestation. This is true also of the sun, of the sky, of the earth, of all creatures and plants.

One even can say that for primordial man, virgin nature is in a sense paradisal, not because there is no suffering in the natural world—to say that would of course be absurd—but rather because primordial man can see through nature to the spiritual archetypes of which nature is an embodiment. There is pain and death in this mutable world, that is indisputable. Hawk and corn, deer and human beings, all die. But each also embodies spiritual archetypes, some more than others. We see in the flight of the hawk also the flight of the soul; there are wings we see, and there are wings of the soul. The wings we see may one day fall to earth; those of the soul's realm die not but are resolved into their Divine Origin.

The soul's natural home is paradise, which it can see in vision, as Black Elk did in his vision when he was nine years old. He saw, with the eyes of the spirit, nature as it truly is in its paradisal Origin and meaning. Through these eyes of the spirit we find also the human Origin and meaning. But virgin nature reminds us who we really are; she embodies the archetypes that call us back to our spiritual homes and no one who walks alone in the wilderness can remain completely unaffected by her.

It is true that the way Native Americans lived before contact with European civilization did entail suffering in the natural world. People got hurt or sick, and people died. Sometimes winters were hard. Sometimes hunting was difficult or crops failed. But these are fleeting things. By way of compensation, people lived lives surrounded by reminders of their spiritual purpose; people lived their lives bathed in the light of Divine revelation as it is manifested throughout virgin nature and again in their cultures, which reflected the archetypes we see in nature herself.

This is why art and ritual in indigenous cultures is always inextricably bound up with virgin nature, with the symbols of lightning and otter, bear and turtle, hawk and deer, mountains and waters. These symbols remind people of their own and nature's Origin, of the archetypes that both human beings and the natural world reflect. To sing a sacred song, to dance a sacred dance, to wear sacred clothing, to make a sacred journey—all these things and all the actions of daily life as well—in the end remind us that we are paradisal beings and that we have obligations to all that surrounds us. The meaning of tribal culture is not just that indigenous peoples and nature are one; it is that both humanity and nature have a spiritual Origin and meaning.

To the modern world, people, trees, stones, animals, the earth, the sky, the stars, and the waters are all separate, discrete things, but for original peoples, nature and human life are not divisible in the modern sense. This is not to say that one cannot tell the difference between a tree and oneself, of course—that would be absurd. There is, however, a mysterious unity between people and their landscape, between people and the creatures around them. This unity is of a subtle kind, not easily explained. But understanding it is essential if we are to enter into a different awareness of our world. Nature, as we see her from this bluff, is a theophany, a divine revelation filled with timeless power.

To the nature of that power we now turn.

2

Wakan, Orenda, Manitou

You are climbing in the mountains and you come to a high place in which you feel a peculiar sense, something you can't quite define. But here you feel a deep contentment, an inward giving. The place is *wakan*—mysterious. In Western Judeo-Christian tradition there arc no words exactly equivalent to the Lakota *wakan*, to the Iroquois *orenda*, or to the Algonquian *manitou*. Admittedly these words have different connotations, but they have far more in common than any of them have with what might be considered the nearest English equivalents, *sacred* and *soul*. But if we are going to move toward understanding this mysterious power in the landscape, in other creatures, or in holy men, we must first step outside our ordinary understanding of the world and of the soul.

In Judeo-Christian exoteric understanding, there are few words more ambiguous than *soul*. Originally, the Greek word *psyche* meant the soul or that aspect of a being that belongs to the "subtle" or intermediate world between above and below, *between* spirit and matter. We still retain this meaning in the word *psychic*, for example. But in later Christian usage, the word *soul* came to refer ambiguously either to the human spirit or to the psyche, and the ancient distinction of body, soul, and spirit was submerged in a dichotomous "soul and body." Furthermore, soul referred strictly to human beings; for the most part, there was no concept in the West of pervasive subtle, or psychic reality intermediate between body and spirit.

This elision and confusion was unfortunate, for in other traditions there are words that bespeak the manifest subtle power running through all nature. In Chinese tradition, the currents of power surging through microcosmic humans and the macrocosmic cosmos are called *ch'i*. Indeed, there is an entire science of the way these currents manifest themselves in nature and in human life, called *feng shui*. In Sanskrit, the word *prana*, meaning "breath of life," likewise expresses the power circulating through our bodies and through the cosmos around us. As we will see, there is a similar understanding among the original peoples.

But in Judeo-Christian tradition this understanding of the mysterious power surging through nature was attenuated, if not lost. The concept of a "soul" became specific to human beings, though occasionally there were academic arguments about whether animals might be included as having some inferior form of soul as well. Of course, there were exceptions: Meister Eckhart, Jacob Böhme, the Christian theosophers generally affirmed a deeper view of the cosmos and continued the Platonic current in a Western tradition that has much in common with the cosomology and religion of the original peoples. Böhme in particular offered a very complex and visionary understanding of the three worlds: the physical, the subtle, and the transcendent. Nonetheless, there were no doubt very few people in the Western Christian world who were aware of this esoteric current; much more common was the brutal and attenuated mentality of those who slaughtered Delaware men, women, and children by burning them to death in a church on a Sunday, shooting those who tried to escape.

People who were willing to commit such atrocities can hardly be expected to be sensitive to the mysterious currents surging through the natural world. In England during the "enlightenment," one found for the first time in history men and women traveling the countryside destroying the ancient standing stones that marked sacred ley lines, the places where nature's currents run.[5] The same insensitivity to the spiritual connections between human life and nature was carried to the Americas. The "enlightenment" marked an encysting of the Western mentality generally, a closing off against the spiritual awareness of the past, signaled by a railing against the "superstitions" of the traditional and balanced medieval Christian understanding and a fanatical destruction of those peoples and monuments of antiquity that represented a spiritual awareness.

Indeed, here lies the very heart of the American darkness: "civilized" people's brutal treatment of the original peoples and of the natural world in America directly reveals not just a spiritual blindness but an antipathy to the spiritual truths that both the Native Americans and the virgin wilderness body forth. The Lakota Sioux Toyanke Wasté Win put it this way:

> The white men have driven the spirits away. The white man's spirits are very far away. They will not come when called. They cannot be bought with gifts. They do not care for men who are alive. The white man's spirit land is nowhere.[6]

To translate from a sacred language is itself a dubious enterprise, for it is not a matter here only of "spirits" in the connotations of that English word today. Rather, it is a matter of the white man's incomprehension of and even outright hostility both to the ancestors and to the sacred powers manifest in nature.

These sacred powers were known to all the original peoples, and especially to the warriors (Lakota: *hunka*) and to the holy ones. As Sunka Hinte, also Lakota Sioux, expressed it:

> There are some secret things taught to a *Hunka*. These secrets are not good now. They are about the spirits. The spirits will not come now. These are the spirits of the Skies, of the Earth, of the Clouds, of the Thunder, of the Land of the Pines, of the Coming-light, of the Sunset, of the South, of the Winds, of the Waters, of the Flying Things, of the Beasts, of the Insects, of the Growing Things, of the Great Beast, and of the Spider. There are bad spirits also. There are ghosts, and the Man from the Land of the Pines. . . . These spirits come no more to the Indians.[7]

The white man's relentless persecution of the original peoples up to the present day—the deliberate destruction of the native traditions—so subverted spiritual connections that it became increasingly difficult for the original peoples to maintain contact with the spiritual beings surrounding them.

These traditions of spiritual connection between humans and the transcendent are in Sioux called *wakan*. The word *kan,* according to the Lakota Sioux, Miwakan, means "tradition," that which is possessed of spiritual power, mystery. *Wakan* means anything or anyone who is traditionally sacred. But many things are *wakan* in this mysterious world of ours, for *wakan* essentially means "mysterious" or "holy." All spirits—and the holy ones who work with the spirits—are *wakan,* and hence *wakan* can be used both of good and of evil beings, both material and nonmaterial.[8]

We begin to see why the word *wakan* is untranslatable into English: it denotes a fluid concept for which there is no precise equivalent in contemporary English. Yet there is in all Amerindian cosmology nothing more central to our understanding the spirituality of landscape than the words *wakan, orenda,* or *manitou.* Consequently, we need to orient ourselves by reaching back to Western antiquity and finding references in Western Platonic, Christian, and other traditions that can help us understand something of what these words entail.

Most important is the Neoplatonic concept of emanation: in a mysterious way, the original unity—that eternally *is*—divided within itself and began the progressive emanation within itself from the 'nonformal transcendent' to the 'formal', from the spiritual to the physical. This emanation means, to cite Lakota tradition, that the original unity hypostasized into the superior beings, including Wi (sun), Skan (sky), Maka (earth), and Inyan (primal substance or rock) and into the subordinate beings, who include Hanwi (moon), sun's companion; Tate (wind), sky's companion; Unk (contention), earth's companion; and Wakinyan (the winged one), companion of Inyan, the primal substance.

One sees here the primal division of the cosmos, the "opening" within the transcendent necessary for creation to take place. The basis of creation, or existential reality, is Inyan, the primal substance, and this primal substance must "precede" the rest of creation in order to establish a basis, or boundary, which for us is manifested in stone or rock, the "outer limit" of materiality. Between the transcendent and the primal substance, then, the whole range of creation can take place, and this is why Inyan takes a prior place in the traditions of the original peoples; manifested in the stone, or primal substance, Inyan is the primal creative act. This is why the Oneida, for example, are the "people of the Oneida stone." The Oneida possessed in this simple statement the metaphysical truth underlying existence itself. But we will return to the sacred stone later.

An engraving showing the Oneida Stone, New York State. The Oneida Stone is like the Greek omphalos *stones inasmuch as it too represents the center of the cosmos. From Schoolcraft,* History of the Indian Tribes, *1854.*

For our purposes here, it is important above all to recognize that the cosmology of the original peoples corresponds fundamentally to the Platonic and Neoplatonic understanding of the cosmos, and in many ways also to the esoteric understandings of Buddhism, Hinduism, Judaism, Christianity, and Islam. In these traditions, initiates recognize the emanatory nature of our cosmos and of the forces within it. In the space between the 'transcendent' and the 'substance' appear the pairs, or syzygies, that manifest as our present world: Sun and Moon, Sky and Wind, Earth and Contention, the Winged Ones and the Rock. "Within" these powers in turn appear the powers of spirits in their whole range from the greater to the lesser, including the evil ones. In Platonic terms, this hierarchy ranges from the gods to demons to men; in Amerindian terms, the hierarchy is much the same: Creation is a primal emanation.

By virtue of the primal emanation of power that constantly creates the cosmos, everything in nature participates moment by moment in the primal unity, in the celestial mystery of archetypal creation. "Archetypal creation" means that everything we see in the natural world reflects its celestial archetype, its spiritual Origin. Just as Plato recognized this truth with his concept of celestial Forms, so too the original peoples recognized it in their religion and mythology. For example, the buffalo is not just an animal but is instinct with the spirit of the buffalo. Thus the buffalo, or the tree, or the rock, is a physical thing that also functions as spiritual revealer.

For modern people, of course, a rock is merely a rock, or at best a fetchingly pretty rock. But for the original peoples, a rock can represent the fundamental act of creation. Pahuru, a rocky outcropping sacred to the Pawnee, is indeed a rock—but it is also, simultaneously, a manifestation of the spirit of the rock and the place where the spirits of the animals congregate. This metaphysical and cosmological awareness of the original peoples is why their mythologies speak, for instance, of a hunter traveling along and seeing what might be translated as a "magical rock," the spirit of which divulges a truth to him. That rock is not mere matter that acts as an abode for a spirit, as we might try to conceive of it; rather, the rock is a manifestation of its transcendent origin, of its spiritual archetype, and that archetype reveals a truth to the hunter. For modern people, who think in dichotomies, there is a spirit and there is a rock; for the original peoples, the rock bodies forth its archetype. All things in nature can act as spiritual revelation.

We have difficulty understanding this, in part because of the confusion engendered by the degeneration of the word *soul* in English. Where once soul meant "subtle energy," it came to signify an "individual." But if we consider *soul* as "subtle energy," then the word also adequately indicates part of what is meant by the word *orenda*. For it is not that an elk "has a soul." Rather, first there is a celestial archetype of Elk, then the subtle energy surging through the being, and then the elk we actually see, which here moves and has its birth, life, and death. All of this is *wakan*.

Once we understand the fundamentally hierarchic nature of the cosmos, it is then possible to understand something of the full range of meanings— from "holy" to "subtle energy" to "subtle being," depending upon the particular construction or use—signified by the words *wakan*, *orenda*, and *manitou*. Thus a holy man before a sacred dance can say that "everything has a spirit. . . . A prairie dog has two spirits: a spirit like a tree, and a spirit like the breath of life."[9] By this he means that an animal is a spiritual archetype as well as the subtle energy that bodies forth that archetype.

Now all this means that to invoke the spiritual archetype of the Buffalo is to invoke *wakan*, to invoke that which originates the buffalo we see, the mysterious energy of the many buffalo. Indeed, the buffalo Spirit can impart traditional teachings and spiritual revelations to the individual warrior or holy man. So too can the Rock Spirit or any other transcendent being. And it also means that one can affect the subtle energy of a particular being: this is the essence of magic. One can add to or diminish the subtle energy of a person, an animal, indeed, of anything in creation. Here is the essence of healing and of killing.

This is not to say that every creature or place or object is equally a manifestation of spiritual and subtle power, of *wakan, orenda, manitou.* The high place in the mountains to which we have come manifests more spiritual power than most places; in it one feels the subtle energy of the rocks and of the sky gathered, and in it we are closer to the origin of things. The same is true of some animals, of some objects, of some people.

Let us summarize. When we found this place in the mountains, we felt a certain ambience that came not just from the view of the surrounding countryside but from our awareness of a mysterious power within it. Although it may seem that we may direct this mysterious power, it is more accurate to say that it directs us. Encompassing the widest implications of the English words *soul* and *spirit, wakan* refers to holiness or sacredness manifested in the world around us, and to the hierarchic, emanatory nature of our cosmos perhaps best understood by reference to Platonism. There are archetypal spiritual powers, and those powers in turn manifest themselves in what we see around us, in individual beings. But understanding this truth means understanding the nature of timelessness and time, to which we now turn.

3
Timelessness and Time

In order to understand America as spiritual landscape, it is necessary for us to abandon modern notions of time. In the modern world, history is valorized; we want to date every event, and we absurdly believe—in the face of the destruction of nature and religious traditions everywhere—that we are "evolving" toward some kind of ideal historical state, caught in historical currents we seem convinced represent not destruction but progress. From the primordial understanding of the Native American traditions, however, this idolization of history is recognized as the absurdity it is. For in truth, in order to enter into the spiritual landscape of America, it is necessary first of all to relinquish the concept of linear history and to understand cyclical, regenerative time as a reflection of eternity.

Essentially, the modern view of time is positivist, relentlessly limited to the historical. This obsession with dates and with linear, measurable time, however, is aberrant by comparison to the understanding manifested in the world's religious traditions generally. It is often said that Asian religious traditions are singularly unconcerned with historical dates, and that this unconcern disturbs many Western scholars. But from a religious perspective,

21

the appearance of a Shakyamuni Buddha or a Nagarjuna is not a historical event but a spiritual revelation. What modern people are so obsessed with—dates, historicity—is in the traditional view merely a reflection of metaphysical or spiritual reality, and only this reality is ultimately significant.

The Western fixation with historicism results, to be sure, from the progressive modern blindness to the spiritual that appeared in conjunction with rationalism, scientism, and, not coincidentally, the European colonization of the New World. One could well say that the European colonization of the Americas represented a physical manifestation of the spiritual blindness at its heart. Emblematic of this spiritual blindness was Coronado's journey into the heart of America: he came to "Quivira," a spiritual center and from the Amerindian perspective, an earthly paradise—but physically seeking "seven cities of gold," he could not see where he was; he sought only plunder. Limited to historical reality, he could not see or understand the spiritual significance of what surrounded him in the New World. This blindness is at the heart of the modern viewpoint throughout all our experiences in the Americas.

Modern people's historicism in part derives from what amounts to a secularization of Christian historocentricity. Through medieval times, Christianity was able to maintain simultaneously a cyclical and a linear view of history; if on the one hand one has the expectation of time's end, and the Second Coming at the "end of history," on the other hand, one has in Christianity also the quadripartite cyclicity seen in the four gospels, the four symbols representing them, and their astrological or seasonal calendrical revolutions seen too in the Books of Days. But in modernity, Christianity as a spiritual totality became weakened and fragmented, and from this ambience came the degenerate or secularized views of history seen in Marxism and in Keynesian capitalism, not to mention evolutionism and Teilhardism. All of these represent the exclusion of metaphysical and cosmological cyclic reality.[10]

By contrast, the Amerindian traditions understand time primarily in metaphysical and cyclical terms. For them, timeless spiritual revelation is at the heart of our place in this world; it is the metaphysical center of our being. The rhythmic cycles of nature reflect this metaphysical heart; in the seasonal, directional, and astrological patterns of nature we see the cosmological reflection of their metaphysical or spiritual Origin. Nature's cycles turn in an endless, harmonious round, which human beings have their axial place in maintaining and which exist so that individuals can realize in those patterns their metaphysical Origin and meaning. Nature turns us toward the Divine.

Hence, in the Amerindian, as in the Mahayana and Vajrayana Buddhist traditions, both spatiality and temporality alike are transmuted, recognized in their archetypal, transcendent essence. In both Native American and Vajrayana Buddhist traditions, directionality is transmuted: west, north, east, and south are all recognized in imaginal or archetypal reality as transcendent Powers or Beings—as are the four semicardinal directions, the zenith, the nadir, and the center. With each of these transcendent directional Powers or Buddhas are very specific color, elemental, gestural, and other symbolic correspondences, all of which taken together represent the realization, from the human perspective, of transcendent reality.

When spatiality is recognized in its archetypal or essential nature, temporality correlatively passes away; the corruptible is recognized as an illusory manifestation of the eternal Divine. In essence, the visionary realization of directional symbolism is entry into archetypal, imaginal reality in which time in our historical, or linear, sense no longer exists. This is not to say that there is no time whatever in imaginal reality but rather that its nature is fundamentally different than that which we experience in the corporeal world.

This sense of timelessness is directly experienced in visions. It is common for visionaries to say that two days, four days, a week, even twelve days passed during the vision—but timelessness is indirectly experienced through tribal rituals as well. Indeed, there is a direct continuity between visions and rituals, for the rituals reflect the visions in which they were presented to the tribe; rituals are an acting out in the physical world of visionary reality, a reaffirmation of human and natural Divine Origins. A tribal ritual—building a sacred lodge, holding a certain kind of dance—is a way of manifesting in the physical world its archetypal or celestial origins. A ritual is not timeless in the sense that it never changes, but it is timeless in that it is a changing reflection in our corporeal world of the incorporeal or transcendent reality.

Another sense of timelessness can be seen in the cyclical nature of rituals. Just as the seasons turn one into another, just as the sun and the moon follow their rising and falling, just as the stars turn around the north, just as planets appear and disappear in the night sky, so too rituals recur, reinforcing the natural cycles without which we could not live. In ritual, people assume their mediate positions in the cosmos, revealing that the archetypal continues to manifest itself in the physical world, that the Buffalo Spirit appears in thousands upon thousands of buffalo, that nature's rhythms bodying forth the eternal continue.

In other words, ritual enacts and thereby reaffirms the cyclical nature of the cosmos; in ritual, we humans see our place in the temporal cycles as a whole. Paradoxically, then, what appears to us as the changing panoply of seasons and natural cycles is also and simultaneously a reaffirmation of timelessness, for the rhythmical cycles represent changing patterns of the unchanging, the mystery of life itself. This cyclicity is not limited to the four seasons but extends far beyond a single year—for in Amerindian traditions, as in Hindu, Buddhist, and other esoteric traditions, the longer cycles of time in which we live are also recognized.

In Hinduism and Buddhism—as also in Greek, Roman, Judaic, Christian Hermetic, and Islamic traditions—one finds reference to the "four ages," sometimes identified with the metals gold, silver, bronze, and iron and sometimes with the four legs of the sacred cow or with the Pythagorean *tetraktys.*[11] These four ages begin with a paradisal Golden Age and end with the conclusion of the Iron Age, which is full of strife, suffering, and destruction. Currently, we live in the Iron Age, known in Hindu tradition as the Kali Yuga. But this quadripartite time cycle—though far longer than current historical records—is still only part of much longer time cycles, some record of which is retained within Buddhist, Hindu, and Islamic traditional sources.

One sees a similar cyclical understanding of time in Amerindian traditions generally, and in Hopi traditions particularly. According to the Hopi, there are four worlds, the first of which was Tokpela, or "infinite space." Its color was yellow; its metal was gold; and its inhabitants were happy together for a very long time, until finally some became destructive, and the Creator decided to save some of the people and destroy the rest. Those he saved went on to populate the second world, Tokpa, whose mineral was silver. In this world, too, people became greedy and destructive, ignored the Divine, and finally once again a few religious people went into the "womb of the earth," in an ant kiva, while the second world was destroyed by ice. The people then emerged into the third world, Kuskurza, where the mineral was copper, and were for a time happy. Once again, however, at the end of the cycle, people grew acquisitive and irreligious, using magical power in very destructive ways—and so there came a purifying flood. To survive this flood, the religious people floated in hollow reeds above the waters and came to rest upon the highest mountain. Finally, they were led by Spider Woman to the current fourth world, Tuwagachi, the metal for which is "mixed."[12]

There are several things to note about this "myth of the Emergence," common in slightly different forms to many tribes, particularly those of southwestern North America. Above all, we need to note that the Emergence is not a hidden tribal reference to evolutionism; humankind is not "evolving" toward a common "New Age." Rather, the myth of Emergence refers to the doctrine of time cycles found throughout the world's religious traditions; each of the four worlds represents a single time cycle within a larger cycle to which we belong, and each of the catastrophes represents the obliteration of decadent past civilizations, some of which were destroyed because they had decayed into very destructive forms of sorcery. The catastrophe at the end of our own age will be the most complete, for its end represents the conclusion both of a single cycle and of a larger quadripartite cycle.

We should note also that the symbolism involved is not a progressive ascent from an inferior to a superior state; rather, humans are born into a primordial "golden" or paradisal world; humankind slowly becomes decadent; the decadent ones are destroyed; and a new world appears, at its inception more perfect than the last at its decadence but not as perfect as the first age. Hence what we must here call "metahistory" is a downward spiral, each spiral returning to the same relative place in the circle but slightly lower. And the human state of Emergence into the world from the ant kiva or the hollow reeds represents the reemergence from the "heart of the world" of primordial man, which is precisely the symbolism also of Noah's ark upon the floodwaters.

We may at first be confused by the Hopi use of apparently spatial symbolism to depict temporo-spatial realities; but although the symbolism corresponds to the particularities of Hopi life in some respects, its fundamental nature is not different from Buddhist and Hindu traditions regarding the end of a time cycle and the planting of seeds "carried on celestial winds" from the end of one age in the beginning of the next. Individual beings do not reincarnate in a New Age; this literalistic interpretation of religious truths has evolved only because we live in an era limited almost completely to the materialistic. Rather, an entire time cycle begins anew, only causally connected to the last cycle.

Essentially, then, the Amerindian view of the world understands time as a series of spirals or cycles and therefore entails regarding life in its seasonal nature rather than as a line that passes from birth to death. This cyclicity is the temporal reflection of the eternal, and to live one's life within the turning of cycles obliterates the concept of progress. Modern people seek to justify materialistic acquisitiveness by speaking of "evolution" and "progress"; we believe, via what one might call a secularized version of Christian historocentrism, that in a linear future will appear the solutions to the destruction we cause today. By contrast, the original peoples live their lives in the light of the eternal.

Imagine, for a moment, how the Amerindian peoples experienced the world before the coming of white people. A generation of people would come and go, and come again on the earth, like the grass or the buffalo or the leaves on the trees—and the earth remained the same. One learned the language and the religion and the ways of one's ancestors; one lived one's life in the cycle of rituals and seasons and ages that were all understood in light of the sacred. There was no need to acquire great technological power or money, nor was there a need to destroy the earth; such things were quite literally inconceivable. To die in such a world is no great tragedy: the seasons turn; the spiral comes around again; the eternal is everywhere present.

Then comes modern civilization, with our blindness to the sacred, with our inability to simply live in this gift that is the sacred earth. From the beginning modern people have been time-bound creatures. We have dates for everything; we even date the creation of artificial boundaries like states or the first "expedition" into land that had been occupied for millennia. In a sense, this preoccupation with history and linear time is comical; in another sense it is tragic. It was not just the concept of individually owning the earth that was foreign to the Amerindian peoples; the modern concept of linear time was even more alien.

To a people who lived in eternal cyclicity, the concept of historicity represents a terrible fall from grace, a fall into time, one might say. It is no wonder that Amerindian peoples have faced great difficulty when forced to live under the modern understanding of humanity's place in the world, when forced to leave the sacred and live in a secular world. Yet not all the Amerindian peoples have succumbed; it is true that there is terrible poverty and suffering among them, but even while dispossessed, expulsed from the

Garden, thrown into modern history, they still retain their awareness of the quadripartite, ever-turning wheel of time and space.

Meanwhile, bombarded by a sense of history, trapped in a world of entertainment and of ever-faster rushing time, modern civilization is ever more unlikely—as a whole—to reestablish links to sacred traditions, to recover an awareness of the eternal and of its reflection in the spirals of seasonal time. Nonetheless, the seasons continue their turning, the stars and planets continue in the sky, the waters, earth, animals, plants, and stones still remain. Spiritual truth has not vanished; humanity's place on earth is not gone, it is only eclipsed for a while. From the high places, religious people still call out the holy songs, calling individuals back to their Origin. For we are each called back to spiritual truth alone; we each must make our way to spiritual realization for ourselves. Although humanity en masse may rush headlong into its own obliteration, an individual may still turn about and walk the ancient ways. Although caught in this, the ending of an age, we may each enter still the sacred and timeless, which is never gone. The turning cycles of time wheel on, reflecting the eternal light of which they are the manifestation and in which we live, whether we know it or not.

4
Totemic Revelations

Everywhere one looks in the Americas, one finds the greatest diversity in the native religious traditions, and yet underlying that diversity, fundamental truths are everywhere the same. Indeed, perhaps nowhere on earth has there been at once such widespread cultural unity and diversity as among the original peoples of the Americas. One is dazzled by the vastness, by the many languages and customs and traditions, so much so that some contemporary authors have taken to claiming that there is little or no underlying unity. But, in fact, the traditions of the original peoples—rooted as they are in the transcendent beauty and spiritual truth of virgin nature—are each adaptations to a particular locality or spiritual landscape. This manifestation of the universal in a particular locale is particularly evident in totemic revelations.

Ohiyesa, a Sioux, writes about totems:

Ever seeking to establish spiritual comradeship with the animal creation, the Indian adopted this or that animal as his "totem," the emblematic device of his society, family, or clan. . . . The sacred beast, bird, or reptile,

28

represented by a stuffed skin, or by a rude painting, was treated with reverence, and carried into battle to insure the guardianship of the spirits.[13]

A totem essentially signifies the archetypal kinship of the natural and the human worlds; its signs are reminders of—or, to put it another way, a grounding in—this archetypal kinship.

There is in one sense a great range in the ways different tribes or peoples view totems, spiritual archetypes, and clans. In most tribes, one has a particular totemic affiliation, and that affiliation—with the bear, say—then is mediator between the transcendent and the earthly; one is the Bear archetype, and the bear embodies for that person spiritual revelation. On the other hand, in other tribes, one at times is enjoined to invoke all spiritual beings at once. This is particularly true, under special circumstances, among the Winnebago and the Ojibway.[14] But in both cases, one is enjoined to recognize that the natural world is spiritual revelation—and in any case, to seek one spirit guardian as mediator to all others, or to seek the simultaneous guardianship of all spirits, are not concepts that are fundamentally opposed but represent differing aspects of the same thing.

Essentially, in totemic revelation we see *kathenotheism*. That is, in general, tribal peoples recognize many spirits, but in a particular revelatory instance one spirit manifests a link to that totality—and for that revelation represents in a sense all spiritual power. This corresponds in many ways to ancient Asian religious traditions: one who worships Kali, for instance, is in Hindu tradition worshiping the totality of spiritual transcendence as manifested in that one goddess. The seeking of a single spiritual revealer therefore does not contradict the recognition of all other spirits as well.

In the Algonquian traditions, for instance, one encounters this concept in the words of a Fox: "There is no difference between a bear and one who goes by the name of a bear; both are one and the same. The fox and a member of the Fox clan are one and the same person. The fox is guardian to all those who bear the Fox name."[15] This means that the spiritual archetype of the Bear or the Fox acts as entryway into the totality of spiritual experience for the person affiliated with that clan. This is why the various medicine bundles of different tribes are in general held under the spiritual auspices of a particular archetypal revealer; the bundle represents cosmological affiliations linked to an archetypal nexus.

A totemic bundle is a grounding of a spiritual experience, a direct connection between a spiritual revelation and the physical and psychic world. In the bundle—kept hidden from view, wrapped in a sacred covering—are objects that, transfigured by the spiritual revelation they embody, mark and emanate its essence. In witchcraft, the practitioner seeks to capture the essence of someone or something for acquisitive or destructive purposes; in the sacred bundle, one carries the embodiment of the healing spiritual revelation granted by a particular spirit or group of spirits. If it be a bear spirit, then one might carry in the bundle bear claws, a bear's ear, and other sacred objects that vehicle the bear spirit's power.

Although some museums possess the sacred bundles of different tribes, those bundles—placed in such a setting—have lost their numinosity, have become curiosity pieces. Individual totemic bundles are said to lose their force after a generation even in ritually supported circumstances, and deprived of the unitary context of a tradition—without reverence and ritual and the renewal of spiritual practice and experience—even the holiest of bundles loses much of its significance and power.

Tribal people are affiliated with a clan not because—as some commentators have suggested—they saw the creatures in that area and turned them into deities but because the particular animals in a given vicinity are manifestations of spiritual archetypes and are therefore revealers of both cosmological and metaphysical truth. Some modern commentators have proposed that clan traditions among various tribes served only to eliminate inbreeding, for it was virtually universally held that people whose totem was the same could not intermarry. But this prohibition in fact has a spiritual origin as well: although in the physical world, members of one species under normal circumstances do not turn into or breed with members of another[16]— because the spiritual archetype that engendered them is different—people whose archetypal guardians are the same are spiritually members of the same family and so are prohibited from incest.

In any myth, we see a fundamental spiritual truth expressed by means of images, and in Native American mythology we find the spiritual origin of the totem also expressed mythically. Ohiyesa speculates that "it is probable that [one's totem] was the traditional ancestress, as we are told that the First Man had many wives among the animal people."[17] Certainly, in the myth of the First Man taking wives among the "animal people" we can see the archetypal unity between man and the animal kingdom. Both reflect the same fundamental spiritual Origin; they are spiritual kin.

There are clearly, in the various tribal traditions, different kinds and levels of totemic spirits and of spiritual revelation, ranging from those of herbal medicine and physical healing through those of the chivalric revelation of the warrior to those of the shaman's transcendent revelations.[18] Herbal medicine entails a knowledge of the subtle realm, of plants and the properties they represent, but one need not be a holy man to understand that kind of cosmological knowledge. The warrior is enjoined to attain direct knowledge of transcendent truth beyond the changeable subtle realm, to attain a vision of the transcendent that encompasses all the powers and principalities above him. But the shamans act as caretakers for all the levels of knowledge and are charged with maintaining spiritual knowledge in its totality.

It is often repeated that in the Plains tribal traditions, everyone in the tribes was enjoined to seek visions and to experience the divine powers directly. This is true—but it does not mean that in other tribal traditions most people were cut off from that kind of direct experience. Across all of the Americas, among the whole range of tribal peoples, each individual participated in a spiritual reality that meant anyone might receive a spiritual vision or a revelatory dream.[19] And, in fact, the vision or dream of an individual, as revelation, might very well reveal a ceremonial context in which individual dreams and visions played a central part: each individual directly experienced a reality known to the rest of the tribe.

This interrelationship between individual and tribal spiritual awareness can be illustrated in countless ways. During a time when the earth had become *ngamwin,* "unstable"—that is, spiritual awareness of the tribe was weakened—the Delaware were given the Great Lodge Ceremony in a dream experienced by one individual, who with great precision explained the dimensions and orientation of the Great Lodge.[20] That Lodge then became the center of vision and dream recitation for the old men, and then for the younger men and women. In other words, through an individual dream came a ceremony reaffirming the spirituality of the tribe as a whole—and that ceremony in turn became a forum for the relating of individual dreams and visions reaffirming the spiritual awareness of the tribe.

Likewise, one finds that among the Pawnee, during each winter buffalo hunt one of the best warriors would have a vision in which he was instructed to perform the spring buffalo ceremony. This visionary would then call in the five priests—of the four semicardinal directions and of the Evening Star—

who would affirm his vision and give him instructions. Following a sacred ceremony in the spring, and throughout the summer, the visionary would be dressed in a special buffalo robe. During the tribe's migration, the visionary would have to remain in his robe and refrain from washing, bathing, handling knives, scratching himself, stepping in water, or participating in acts of violence.[21]

In essence, the visionary had come to embody Paruksti, the Wonderful Power, the Thunderstorm, the Primal Energy. Consequently, what he did affected not only the tribe but the entire locale. If he stepped in water, there would be terrible storms. If he grew angry or thought bad thoughts, tribesmen would be hurt on the buffalo hunt. Wrapped in his robe like sacred corn in its husk, the visionary had been granted a great blessing, entwined with which was great danger as well, not only for him but for the entire tribe and indeed for their whole world.[22]

One sees here again how indivisibly intertwined are the individual visionary experience, the tribal destiny, and the cosmic cycle. The warrior who is instructed to embody Paruksti takes on for a time a suprahuman role: he, the tribe, and the natural world they inhabit are all vehicles for transcendent or divine power, which directs them. Yet the warrior as vice-regent for that power can err; he is a vehicle and as such can conduct the power well or can err in his conduct. If he errs, however, the consequences for tribespeople or for the natural world can be very great.

A ritual tradition like that of the Pawnee is a spiritual revelation indivisible from the cosmic cycles manifesting in the natural world; it is a revelation, however, not mediated through a clan's totem but rather is manifested to the tribe as a whole. The totemic revelations corresponding to medicine bundles, for instance, are spiritual revelations to particular clans; the ritual visionary tradition of the Pawnee is a revelation to an entire tribe. The same relationship prevails among all the different tribes of the original peoples: the individual dream or vision is not really individual at all but rather is a particularized manifestation of the transcendent power that guides all the tribespeople.

But even though only one hunter each year is chosen among the Pawnee to be the particular embodiment of the primal power, in many tribal traditions each young man went out to fast and seek a vision or dream, and from very early childhood, children were often asked their dreams by their mothers. This is only another way of saying that among all these peoples, spirituality is not reserved for one or another class, but was open to all; everyone participated in a world that embodied spiritual significance.

"Embodied" must be emphasized here: the vision or dream is in essence a grounding of the spiritual, as well as its irruption into the subtle, dreaming world; this is why in so many traditions it is necessary to enter into a ritualization of the dream or vision. One may leave a mark in the form of a petroglyph; or one may, in returning to the tribe and one's family, participate in an elaborate guessing game in which other people become aware of the dream; or one may act it out for others in a ceremonial retelling; or in rare cases, one may have been granted a revelation of a new ceremony for the entire tribe. In all these cases, the dream or vision is an irruption of the spiritual into the physical world and must be assimilated into the psychic life of the people.

To this day, there are those among the various tribes who travel to the ancient sacred places and pass the night offering smoke and tobacco, singing, and then dreaming—perchance of an animal spirit, perchance of one of the anthropomorphic spirit-beings, seen as surpassingly beautiful men or women.[23] The sacred place to which one travels might be a high hill, or a sacred mound or embankment or a place marked by petroglyphs— the particular tradition determines one's visionary site, which in turn provides the ambience in which the spirit or spirits most easily manifest. A rock drawing of a spirit-being signifies a place in which that spirit has manifested before and, in a sense, is that spirit; there is a continuity of experience.

Totemic revelation is linked indivisibly to the native spirituality of the Americas and marks the joining of heaven and earth. It is no accident that the seekers of visions go to the high hill or to the mountain, for there they are lifted up by the very earth and stand midway between earth and the heavens; there the natural world is laid out below and around them, and they are indeed the link between above and below, between the spiritual and the physical. It is no accident, either, that what the visionary has seen appears in marks upon the rock; for the rock endures, the rock is the oldest of all earthly creations, and on it appears not the impress of human fantasy, but a reminder for those who come after of the archetypal spiritual reality that has been, is, and always shall be.

The totemic revelation—spiritual revelation in the context of America's original peoples—is not merely the manifestation of "primitive" people's desire to manipulate a physical world they imperfectly understood because they had not "evolved" to our current state of "technological sophistication." Rather, the totemic revelation, considered in its totality and as a spiritual phenomenon, reveals to us the astonishing unity of spiritual, psychic, and physical, of metaphysics, cosmology, and natural cycles found in the traditions preserved by the original peoples of the Americas.

5
Sacred Man
and the Great Mystery

In order to understand any religious tradition, one has to recognize not just what fallen man represents within its context but what man *can be* as well. For all authentic traditions reveal to humanity the divine archetype of universal man, of man not as suffering being but as the one who bears within himself or herself the archetypal, universal possibilities for being human. In Eastern Christianity, this universal man is called *theanthropos,* which means "divine one" and is embodied in Christ—to whose illumined station all religious beings aspire. So too with Buddhism, one sees in the Buddha, seated in meditation, the very archetype of serenity, energy, and transcendent illumination. Indeed, every tradition has its image of the station to which humanity aspires, of illumination and liberation incarnate. But how is this station—how is the theanthropos—represented in primordial Native American traditions?

There are of course some means of pictorial representation within the various Amerindian traditions: one finds figures etched on stone, drawn on birchbark, painted in sand, or carved from wood all across the Americas. But nowhere in Native American traditions does one find iconic representation of a theanthropos in the fashion of an Eastern Christian iconic representation of Christ or of a Buddhist representation of Shakyamuni Buddha. In part this is because there is in the Amerindian traditions no theanthropic figure of universal man as redeemer as there is within the Buddhist, Christian, Judaic, Muslim, or Hindu traditions.[24]

Indeed, the Native North American traditions are in general renewed not by a single avatar but by what might be called a cultural diffusion of the avatar: one or another tribal member has a vision, and in this is revealed the ceremonial event or religious practice necessary to renew the tradition. What is more, spiritual practices—fasting, seeking a vision, interpreting dreams—are open to the tribe as a whole and in many cases enjoined upon them. All this means in the North American traditions that the function of theanthropos, or universal man, rather than being revealed in a single incarnation or in multiple incarnations, is in a certain sense—potentially at least—revealed to or in everyone in the tribe.

This universalization of the theanthropos —if one may so call it—corresponds to early Buddhism in that both are aniconic, or without representations of the universal man. For in early Buddhism, one finds only aniconic or symbolic representations of the Buddha—footprint images, eight-spoked wheels, and other symbols—but no images of Shakyamuni Buddha himself.[25] This aniconism derives in part from the tradition's temporal proximity to the Teacher himself: each disciple is enjoined to realize the Dharma for himself, and the revelation's power is still strong.[26] So too in Amerindian traditions, each individual is called to realize spiritual truth for himself; there is no redeemer.

Of this tradition—in Lakota Sioux called *hanblecheyapi,* or "lamenting for a vision"—Black Elk said,

> Anyone can cry for a vision, or "lament"; and in the old day we all—men and women—"lamented" all the time. . . . There are many reasons for going to a lonely mountaintop to "lament." Some young men receive a vision when they are very young and when they do not expect it, and then they go to "lament" that they might understand it better. Then we "lament" if we wish to make ourselves brave. . . or to prepare for going on the warpath. Some people "lament" in order to ask a favor of the Great

Spirit . . . and then we also "lament" as an act of thanksgiving for some great gift which the Great Spirit has given us. But perhaps the most important reason for "lamenting" is that it helps us to realize our oneness with all things, to know that all things are our relatives.[27]

In order to fast and cry for a vision, one takes the *inipi,* or sweat bath, and one talks to a priest, or holy man. The *inipi* is purification; the holy man is one's guide.[28]

The sweat-lodge ceremony is a spiritual purification and rebirth for the participant. The lodge is said to be like a mother's womb, and furthermore, because of the rocks and the fire and the water, it represents a microcosm in which are all the primal elements of Creation. The *inipi* ceremony is necessary in order to purify and to make sacred those who pass through it. In the firepit are placed seven stones, which represent not only the four directions but the three realms (physical, subtle, and celestial) as well; the seven stones are also seen to be the "seven sisters" of the Pleiades.[29] To enter the lodge is to enter into the primordial Creation, and to emerge is to emerge reborn as primordial man.

The holy man, or *wicasa wakan,* is necessary as a guide for the vision seeker not only because he can give instructions and act as interpreter afterward, but because during the vision-seeking itself he generates and maintains a connection to the seeker, protecting him or her from demonic forces. It is true that every person seeks a vision alone—but one seeks under the auspices of the tribe's sacred inheritance and ambience; one seeks a vision granted by mysterious spirits, the general characteristics of whom are known by the holy man. The *inipi* purifies the "breath of man," which is to say the soul.

The seeker goes to the top of a high hill, to a sacred place from which the rim of the world can be seen, and stays there for up to several days and nights, fasting, confronting directly the fact of human desire, and overcoming it by sheer will or courage. In olden times, some would fast for up to twelve days. The sacrifice entailed by the fast, as well as the sheer concentrative power required to ignore the heat or the cold, the wind or the rain, not to mention hunger and thirst, meant that one or more spirits would take pity on the seeker. The vision-seeking in this regard corresponds in some ways to the Japanese Rinzai Zen Buddhist *sesshin,* or intensive *zazen* retreat, in which participants—under the guidance of the *roshi,* or venerable teacher—sit in meditation for many hours a day, for seven days, and do not speak during the entire time. Like the *sesshin*, vision-seeking represents a manifesting of spiritual power for the benefit of all beings, not just for the seeker.[30]

Indeed, one may well say that seeking a vision entails a concentering of the being on the spiritual heart and a stripping away of illusions; the individual realizes his or her own insignificance in the face of spiritual revelation at the heart of being. Consider the symbolism of lamenting: one strips down, is purified in the sweat lodge through ceremonial means, travels to a high place, and sets out the four poles that mark the fasting place as holy ground. Sitting in the center, without food or water, naked during the day, one has physically removed all the supports for life and is dependent upon the higher powers as is a little child: one's whole effort has been toward the pure, primordial center, toward the heart of being, toward realizing to the extent possible theanthropos, divine or universal man.[31]

Here one encounters the divine mystery in the purest degree that is humanly possible—for here the sacred supports for religious practice keep one safe within the sacred space marked by the poles.[32] One's vision quest is protected by the power of the tradition and of the holy man under whose guidance one is lamenting. Here—if conditions are right and one is indeed prepared—alone in virgin nature, one comes face to face with the divine mystery clothed in a revelatory form.[33]

One finds the practice of fasting for a vision not only in the many Sioux sources but, in fact, all the way across North America, among tribes as diverse as the Iroquois, the Algonquin, the tribes of the Southwest, the tribes of Central America, and the tribes of the West and North as well. Indeed, in 1530, Captain Antonio de Herrera noticed this tradition of isolation, fasting, and revelation among the people of Central America, although as one might expect, he attributed the Central American indigenous spiritual practices to the devil and to a desire for obtaining material goods through supernatural means.[34] Despite the limited insight of the European explorers, however—whose accounts are, alas, often all that remains of the traditions they were zealously obliterating—their writings confirm the relative universality of vision-seeking across the Americas.

It is true that seeking a vision—particularly insofar as it entailed the manifestation of a guardian spirit—could be undertaken in terms of succeeding in battle, gaining more goods, or in general ensuring good fortune. All these physical events are conceived as reflections of spiritual gifts, however, not as ends in themselves, as they are seen in modern times. What is more, there is a visionary hierarchy: if certain tutelary or guardian spirits offer mundane rewards, this does not mean that higher revelations are impossible or that these higher revelations can be construed as belonging to a lower level.

Kagagengs, an Ojibway, for instance, had a premonition that his mother had died. After learning she indeed had, he fell into a state of deep sorrow and mourning. Climbing a tall tree, he hung in the branches and was granted a vision in which he was escorted to the foot of a mountain called "Mountain of the Stag's Heart." There he was shown into the rock, in the center of which was a brilliant being, the Sun. Far below them was the whole earth's rim spread out, all the trees and forests and mountains; above was the vaulted heavens. The Sun-being told him that he would have four sons, that he would live a long life, and that he was granted two guardian spirits, a bird and a white bear. Kagagengs was found in the tree by his four sisters, who, because his spiritual experience was still on him, could not touch him with bare hands. They plucked lime-tree leaves to hold against him—just as he was told in his vision—as they helped him home. He was so weak that it took him three days to recover—just as it was three days' journey undertaken in the tree.[35]

Was this vision "merely an assurance of longevity and of the family's continuation"? Surely it was the profound spiritual experience of Kagageng's life, reverberating at the very heart of his existence. We see in this vision of Kagagengs—told more than one hundred and twenty-five years ago and within the tradition as it was just after white contact—how indivisible are higher and lower, celestial and mundane powers. Daily life and the transcendent vision are of one piece; the totems Kagagengs carried—of the bird and the bear—permeate his daily life with the influence of that singular vision of the Sun.

The vision came as a gift to him after the death of his mother, after the sort of spiritual crisis that many people experience before an illumination. Precipitated by and deeply linked with every aspect of ordinary life, the vision of a Kagagengs—in which he is shown the whole world far below and spread out beneath him—encompasses within it the totality of human life. He sees himself with white hair and four sons; he sees in short the totality of time and space for his existence and the fruition of his life. Illumined by the spiritual Sun, his whole life is vivified by this vision at its center. The vision reveals the heart of his life, in essence the heart of universal man.

One is not surprised to read universally among explorers' accounts—save of those who automatically feared and despised the spirituality they found all about them—that the different tribespeople they encountered were not only physically beautiful, singularly free from disease or defect, but were almost invariably generous, kind, and deeply ethical. Again and again one reads that a stranger would show up at a lodge or tipi and would be welcomed, fed, housed, and cared for without comment or expectation. Indeed, it is well known that in most tribes generosity was prized far and away above wealth; one of the United States government's many despicable policies was, from the late nineteenth century on, to prohibit the Native American peoples' giving away of wealth at funerals or for ceremonial reasons.

One sees all across the Americas the collapse of traditional cultures under the persecution of the whites' antireligious campaigns—not to mention the murders of, thefts from, and outright massacres of Native Americans that to this day have not ceased.[36] There is also a sense in which the original peoples' way of life had already become "old" when the Europeans first contacted them; to say this is in no way to justify the white obliteration of the original peoples, only to point out that at the end of a larger time cycle, certain things are foreordained to happen. The destruction of spiritual traditions (and of nature) is "woven into the fabric" of our time cycle's end.

But there is a great mystery at the heart of human existence that cannot be effaced or blotted out; the purpose and meaning of being human cannot disappear. Even as modern civilization destroys the natural world and all the original peoples, the great mystery remains, and must always remain, at the heart of nature. No matter how deformed we make ourselves, no matter how much we deface the world around us, rendering it sterile and even noxious with toxins, so long as nature exists, so long as the potential for people to realize the Divine remains, our age shall continue.

Spiritual truth, our inheritance, is fundamentally simple. Indeed, we exist for it, not it for us; it informs our earthly existence, whether we know it or not. The end of an age comes when the possibility for spiritual realization is eliminated—so far as this can be so. Far from being the province of one or another people, spiritual realization is the task, the meaning, the purpose of each of us. We are each called to realize universal man to the extent we can; we are each called to the great mystery that brings us, and all beings, forth. This is the message of all religious traditions—Christian, Buddhist, Hindu, Judaic, Muslim, aboriginal[37]—and it is likewise the truth at the heart of the Americas.

Part II
Spiritual Symbolism

INTRODUCTION

To the modern hearer, *symbol* is an abstraction. It indicates that the living being you see—the bear, the glyph upon the rock—merely refers to something else. This is not true. To understand our world in a spiritual way, we need to discard this kind of thinking, for it easily gives rise to the very ratiocentrism that lies at the heart of the modern world and its destructiveness. Moderns do not value the bear or the glyph or the rock at all; we live in a world of abstractions, a bloodless world, a world in which we obliterate an entire landscape to gain the abstraction of money, which is after all nothing but a symbol. If we are going to move toward understanding the spiritual landscape of America, we need to understand what a symbol really means.

To begin, we should not make of our world a series of equations, as though everything we see is the facade of some more abstract reality. This kind of mentality—placing a chasm between material and spiritual reality—has been attributed to the Gnostic Christians, but in fact it is to be seen much more clearly in the modern Western concentration on the physical world. Because as modern Westerners we are schooled on two centuries and more of progressively excluding spiritual truth, having drawn a kind of materialist shell over ourselves, we tend to think of spirituality in contradistinction to the physical world, as something *out there*. This conceptualization of spiritual symbolism effectively excludes one from its inner meaning.

In order to deeply understand a symbol, you must assimilate it; it has to become part of your spiritual geography. To say this is not to deny but to affirm the power of the intellect—intellect not as mere ratiocination but as the supernal light transcending what we call the reason. A symbol divulges its significances slowly and only with sustained concentration; and each symbol's meanings shed light on others. Spiritual symbolism does not exist in isolation from the physical world; rather, it is only in correlation to nature and the spiritual truths she bodies forth that the real nature of spiritual symbolism is revealed. To understand spiritual symbolism is to enter into a visionary landscape. Symbols can only exist in a context, in a totality.

In the discussion that follows I will concentrate on three primary kinds of sacred places: first, rock ledges on which are carved petroglyphs; second, a serpentine glyph carved in the earth; and third, a giant laid out in stones. These sites are all loccated in the Great Plains, but their significance is universal. All of these places are deeply symbolic, but to understand truly what that symbolism means is another matter. Essentially, we at once will be drawing together disparate threads to recover the now-torn fabric of Amerindian traditions, and we will be moving ever further into a visionary understanding of our world. For at heart, all symbols are visionary.

This visionary reality is transmitted to a member of a tribe through the totality of his inherited language, ritual, art, and daily life. Language is paramount in this transmission, for when a myth is related within a tribal context, it is also revealed anew, or to put it another way, it is invoked. The recitation of a myth does not "remind" a tribal member of its truth; the myth exists in timelessness, and its recitation *is* the myth here and now. A primordial language has a mysterious quality of transmission and is indivisible from the reality it invokes. This is why white "civilizers" of Native Americans have tried so hard to destroy the tribal languages and to substitute English, for in this way a profound spiritual link of the tribal peoples is broken. In a broader sense, one may even say that the whole of traditional culture is a kind of language, linking everything one does to spiritual truth.

Those who stand outside these traditional means of invoking, or more accurately, *recognizing* spiritual reality may think that symbols "stand for" something, but this is not true. Rather, what we are calling symbols here are really the spiritual truth embodied, or manifested, before us. To understand what this means in petroglyphs, in terraglyphs, or in other sacred sites may not be so easy, but it is imperative if we are to recognize what it means to live in a spiritual landscape. By understanding spiritual symbolism in this higher sense—as entry into visionary reality—we come to understand something of the real nature of sacred sites and, by implication, of our human place and purpose in this world.

1

Inscriptions in Stone

As you travel southwest through the plains of central Kansas, the hills lengthen out and vistas grow broader: the hills are tan and rolling, the horizon a complete circle. It is as though, as the poet William Stafford has said, the earth lifts you up into the space above it. In a sense, the same phenomenon can happen at a petroglyph site, down near the sacred springs, down in the valleys. One stands before a rock embankment on which are inscribed sacred glyphs and feels lifted up into the realm of the archetypal.

As one travels through the Flint Hills—so called because of the chert deposits just beneath the soil—one sees on the hillsides outcroppings of flaky stone, and along the edges of ridges stones sometimes mark the curves of the land. Farther on in the Smoky Hills, the land turns brown, the vistas wider yet, but down in the valleys the land remains green like oases. There birds sing, water runs, while up on the hills the wind blows across grassy knolls. Occasionally a high bluff stands alone like a noble face. Rivers mark the towns; where there was abundant river water, houses and buildings were placed. But not for the aborigines; for the tribal groups, with their sense of sacred geography, there were other considerations for their village sites.

48

At the time of Coronado's expedition into central Kansas in search of the rumored gold of the Quivira tribe, more than ten thousand people were living in the immediate headwaters of the Little Arkansas River. The population was higher then than it is today, even though this is not rich bottomland by any means. Certainly there were better sites for supporting many people, and one has to wonder why so many were drawn to this area. Why, too, were there rumors of gold and wealth here? Coronado was disappointed; he and his men found only "barbarism" and "poverty."

There are different kinds of wealth, however, and in this headwaters region is a richness of the spirit. Springs have always been sacred; at springs Earth's breath rises, at springs one sees the upwelling of life itself. Here the Earth spirit rises to the surface with a power one does not find in a river lowland; here, amid the grassy knolls and twisting creeks, by the sheer rock outcroppings and the hidden springs, the Earth's spirit manifests herself in the outpouring of the waters.

These are secret places. Petroglyph sites are invisible; on the southern grassy bluff above one sheer rock outcropping, one sees only a line of trees and the suggestion of a winding creek, marked by the green, and beyond is more brown. There is no indication of the mysteries hidden below. If one makes his or her way down among the trees and rocks, however, down the angled face, another world is found, a rocky sandstone ridge jutting north, cool and dark, and along its iron-darkened face are ancient petroglyphs. The springs too are invisible, save through the glimpses of green. Hidden rocks, great rocks beneath the bluffs, are exposed by the meandering creek beds: one feels the power of the stones beneath the earth.

The petroglyphs are on a rock outcropping that runs in a half-moon from southeast to southwest, facing north. To the west, one sees along the outcropping, on a slope that faces northeast, a phallus and a vagina. No doubt many interpreters, influenced by Sir James George Frazer and others, would see these as merely "fertility symbols." But what is a fertility symbol? Is it not more useful to see here the primal representation of male and female in essence—the vagina growing moist like the rains coming in; the phallus like the axis of the world? One can reduce symbols to "merely" this or that meaning, or one can look at how such symbols correspond to primordial human reality. We are concerned here with the opening out, not the closing down, of symbols.

Near where one sees the still-standing walls of a stone barn, and slightly

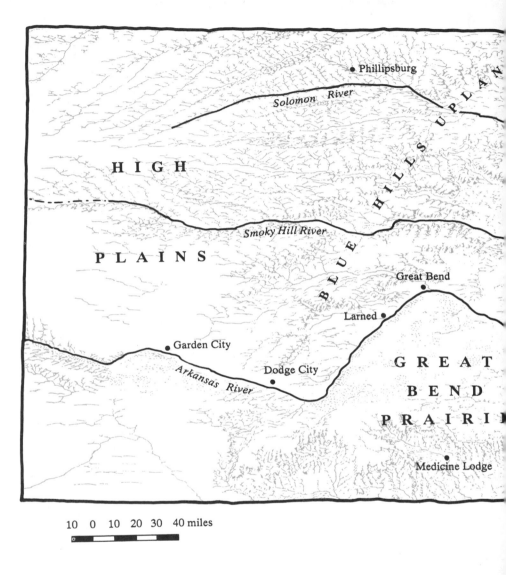

Topography of Kansas, based on a map from the Kansas Geological Survey.

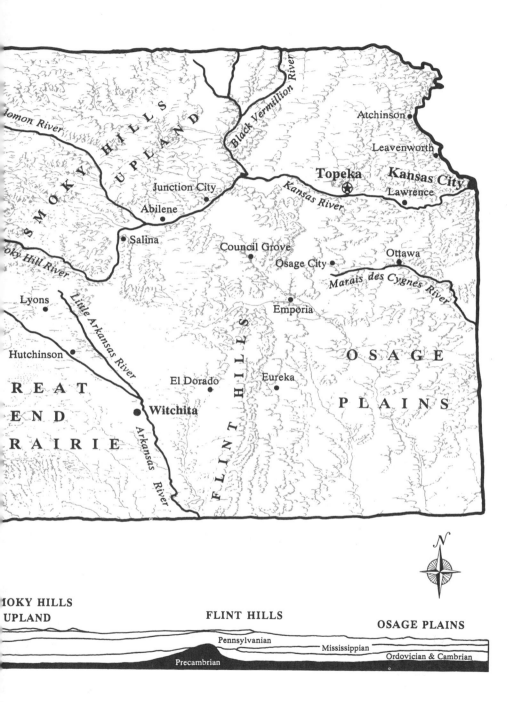

above a ledge carved into the face, is a kind of smooth seat. Directly above or near this seat are a number of petroglyphs, including a famous one showing a concentric circle and a spear, a head and stick feet. Visible on each side of this concentric circle or spiral are the two ends of a spear, on a roughly forty-five degree angle; above it is a round, sketchy head, and below it are two feet. Waldo Wedel has suggested that this insignia represents a shield and a lance held by a warrior, and no doubt this is true. But the "shield" is also, and primarily, a symbol—a symbol that in fact covers the entire body of the warrior and into which his very being is transformed. The warrior, or hunter, has *become* the spiraling power of the shield and the penetrative power of the lance: only his head and his feet (discrimination, or direction, and movement) remain of him as individual. The lance traditionally corresponds to the axis, or pivot, on which things turn.

The shield warrior faces north, the direction from which winter, and often storms, come; beside this insignia, and facing west, is a ladder. In all cultures, the ladder traditionally signifies a change in consciousness: one ascends into the heights or descends into the chthonic depths. In Hopi tradition, the ladder has a cosmological significance as well, in that humankind enters its particular world and time via a celestial emergence. The ladder corresponds to an umbilical cord linking the child and Mother, in this case the spiritually reborn initiate and his or her spiritual Origin.[38] The ladder faces west—the direction of the setting sun and of the western paradise common to Pure Land Buddhism, the Egyptian mystery tradition, and Native American traditions. Perhaps it signifies that the initiate in battle becomes the spiraling and penetrating, or axial, powers; he is reborn, and when he dies, he will enter the western paradise via the spiritual ascent symbolized in the ladder.

Beside and below these hieroglyphs is carved a smooth seat. In the Rocky Mountains, hundreds of miles west, one finds similar seats carved into the stone. Such seats had a ritual function; one would stay in a sacred place marked by hieroglyphs and realize that spiritual power of which the symbols are manifestation. In short, a hidden place like the sandstone outcropping on which these insignias were carved forms a nexus for the contacting of the spiritual powers that inform both ourselves and our world. The carving into the rock of symbols is also a revelation of the powers that are implicitly there to begin with and that the initiatory vision reveals. One is, in such a place, seated symbolically at the heart of the world.

This symbolism is indeed confirmed by a cave with a flue rising directly up into the prairie bluff above the wall of petroglyphs. The flue is axial, and it corresponds both to the world axis and to the "heart line" that connects the head and the heart in many hieroglyphic representations. Below is the cave, the place of darkness and rebirth; above is the light and the blue of the prairie sky. Below is the heart; above is the world of vision, of light and endless space. Earth and heaven, joined by the cave's vertical venting, by the individual heart line.

The sandstone rock outcropping that forms this site is marked on the southwestern edge by a compression of the rock as under enormous force, so that the rock is buckled and wrinkled in narrow, twisted, concentric layers that give the rock face a bizarre, contorted look. This too marks the site as the place of sacred power—the earth herself has manifested her power here and made the rocks show it forth. This is the secret of all the sacred petroglyphs: they are spiritual powers manifesting themselves in the fundamental substrata of earthly existence, in the rocks beneath and before us. There are, of course, such things as trail markers, signs to give tribespeople passing by later an indication of where one went or what one had done. But these are rarely, if ever, found at sacred sites; the sacred petroglyphs are not the products of mere aestheticism nor are they mundane messages among human beings. Rather, the petroglyphs body forth the spiritual powers that inform our cosmos.

When one understands this fundamental truth, the significance of the petroglyph sites becomes clear. They are visionary places, points on our earth at which the veils between the spiritual, subtle, and physical worlds become translucent. There is a cave in central Kansas at which one finds a reclining human figure, and many writers have called this figure "enigmatic." But in fact its nature is clear. Offering an interesting parallel to the famous reclining Buddha figures found in caves in Asia, the cave figure is clearly of initiatory significance. As we have seen, in many tribal traditions, one seeks a vision at a sacred place—often a petroglyph site—and stays there for an extended period of time, fasting and seeking a revelation through a dream or a vision.

Given this tradition of vision-seeking at petroglyph sites, is it surprising to find a figure of a reclining visionary wrapped in a sacred robe, the rays around his head revealing the illuminative sacred power of this site? Is it surprising to see "inside" the visionary the sacred lightning bolt of spiritual power penetrating the entire being, the serpentine power? Lone Man, a

Sioux, explains what he was told by a holy man of his tribe:

> "The earth is large, and on it live many animals. The earth is under [the] protection of something which at times becomes visible to the eye. One would think this would be at the center of the earth, but its representations appear everywhere, in large and small forms—they are the sacred stones. The presence of a sacred stone will protect you from misfortune." He then gave me a sacred stone which he himself had worn. I kept it with me wherever I went and was helped by it. He also told me where I might find one for myself. *Wakan Tanka* tells the sacred stones many things which may happen to people.[39]

The sacred stones in a mysterious way speak to man of his spiritual Origin and offer to him the secrets of his world; they are the fundament of nature, in a mysterious way the Substance that is informed by and reflects the Divine. The same is true of the petroglyph sites.

To this day, Native Americans of many tribes make annual visits to sacred petroglyph sites before undertaking certain rituals like the Sun Dance. As Arthur Amiotte, a Lakota Sioux, put it:

> There offerings are made to the sacred markings. The designs are memorized, brought back, and replicated on the mellowed earth altar. Oddly enough, it is not unusual to find that a certain kind of transformation does take place even today. Year after year the visitation to the sacred site reveals to us that the marks do change, and each year they are in turn brought back and replicated on the sacred altar. Following the Sun Dance proper, the shamans gather together in the purification lodge—the sweat lodge—and interpret those markings in terms of the potential message they might have for the people during the forthcoming year.[40]

One thinks, in this regard, of Moses' stone tablets carried down from the mountain.

The stones and the rock escarpments of this earth are the solid basis upon which we live; they will outlast each of us, and on them sacred power inscribes its symbols. They speak to us of timelessness, of immortality. One contemporary author has written of "teaching stones to talk," but such an attitude is typical of modern people, who want to make the whole world conform to their own patterns, speak their own rationalistic language. Far better to *listen* to the stones and hear what they have to say; only if we are open enough to listen to what the earth's spirits reveal to us will we begin to recognize the spiritual meaning of this world and our place in it.

Nevertheless the sites we have been describing are rarely if at all visited even by the tribespeople who not so many years ago possessed the sacred traditions that authenticated and interpreted the experiences one might have at them. So there is an element of danger in any contemporary visionary practices, for essential to spiritual experience in any tradition is the experienced guide, the master who can distinguish delusion from wisdom, mere madness from insight, and who can interpret wisely what often seems the jumble of the psychic realm.

In visionary experiences, the symbols are not symbols in the ratiocentric sense, for in a vision, as in a dream, the symbol is truly alive in subtle reality. The petroglyphs are manifestations in stone of a reality that transcends the physical realm and informs what we call our world. This revelatory power is what makes the petroglyphs sacred. Like all power, it is dangerous; it is not to be trifled with. But without this revelatory power, what sort of world would we live in?

Of course, at the same time we are faced with the problem of how, precisely, we who are not Native American can approach this kind of spiritual tradition. Some people believe that shifting from one tradition to another is as easy as putting on a different kind of clothing. But the petroglyphs are instinct with specific Amerindian spiritual traditions, and in fact all we who are not of those traditions can do is recognize their beauty and their significance and practice that tradition to which we were born.

Standing here before a great rock wall, the height and breadth of which is inscribed with sacred symbols, do we really believe we can understand its mysteries through reason or through radiocarbon dating? To truly understand these glyphs, we must approach them in humility and with reverence. Even for many tribespeople, the gates of the spirit are closed. This is the nature of our iron age. But if our spirit is earnest, if our intention is strong and good, if we practice our spiritual tradition to the best of our capacity, is it likely that the Divine will withhold from us all spiritual symbolism or the "peace which passeth all understanding"?

2

THE GREAT HORNED SERPENT

The Lyons terraglyphs stand at the headwaters of the Little Arkansas River on a bluff that overlooks a vista to the northwest. To the southeast, you see only the horizon line of a grassy knoll, beyond which is the river itself. To the northwest, you can see the way the valleys slope together, how the springs feed creeks that curve down into the river itself. You are drawn to the northwest by the view; the land itself seems to flow in that direction. Yet the water flows around and to the southeast, behind you, and the storms riding in from the northwest drive in toward you.

The terraglyphs themselves are mysterious. Clark Mallam, a perceptive observer and one of the rare modern investigators with a sense of nature's metaphysical meanings, proposed that the central terraglyph corresponded to the Great Serpent Mound in Adams County, Ohio, which depicts a gigantic serpent holding an egg or sphere in its jaws. The Lyons terraglyph, Mallam suggested, also depicts a serpent holding an egg in its jaws, the angles of which, when extended, form lines that enclose the three council circles, or mounds, one and a half to two miles away, and taken as a whole form a huge single glyph aligned with the summer solstice.

The Lyons Great Horned Serpent; an aerial view of limed terraglyph taken by archaeologist Clark Mallam in 1982. The glyph is roughly 160 feet long and from 3 to 10 inches deep.

One is nonetheless left with questions. A soil subsection showed no evidence of a circle between the jaws, and one wonders how much of the elaborate reconstructions of the site are based on the Great Serpent of Ohio or those in England and elsewhere. Was this really a serpent with a sphere between its jaws? What is more, one sees at the site another, smaller area to the north of the larger terraglyph's northwestern end. This too is serpentine in form, and as one stands at the site, one feels that this too was part of its ritual significance. But because this smaller terraglyph did not fit into the hypothesis of a serpent and an egg, it has been ignored. Indeed, as one gazes into the distant rolling hills, one cannot help but feel that the modern term *serpent* is but a weak reconstruction of this site's ultimate significance.

Yet what was and is that significance? That the form is serpentine is without doubt. So too is the smaller terraglyph north of the larger one—though it curves only left and then back again, formed in a teardrop shape, the larger end to the southwest. Certainly the terraglyphs mark the whole region, for they are found on a high bluff overlooking a whole watershed, and from them one can see for miles. Mallam concluded that most likely

> the intaglio is an early version of the "Giant Horned Serpent, Antlered Serpent, or Water Monster" so common in historic Native American beliefs. Its location on the southeastern margins of the headwaters indicates a "guardian" role for the source of life—water. . . . [The serpent] signified . . . through its placement and orientation, the natural and cyclical process of death, rebirth, and the regenerative power of life. . . . Cross-culturally, the serpent represents . . . "disruption, disharmony, and dissolution," and continual life renewal through annual shedding of its skin and hibernation. It is often associated with earth openings and springs and frequently viewed as the "Chief of the Under (water) World," the "guardian of life-bestowing substances."[41]

As we will see, this interpretation is correct, and has far-reaching implications.

The serpentine form in Native American traditions, as in Hindu, Buddhist, and other religious traditions, is identified with water. Indeed, in Buddhist tradition, as in that of Native Americans, there are said to be serpentine creatures in springs, rivers, and bodies of water, beings in Buddhist tradition called *nagas*. Yet *nagas* are not serpents; they are represented as serpentine in form but are a class of beings that belong to the subtle, or animistic, domain between earth and heaven. Traditionally in Buddhism, *nagas* are regarded as powerful beings who, like dwarves, giants, and other such nonhuman beings, have civilizations or kingdoms of their own, in this case in the waters. In Buddhist tradition it is also said that some scriptures were entrusted to the *nagas* for safekeeping, until human beings descended to a historical state dire enough that they needed the new revelation. It is said that Nagarjuna, for example, was given certain Buddhist teachings by the king of the *nagas*, from which revelation came some aspects of the Mahayana teachings.

In Buddhism, as in Native American traditions, the serpentine being is not regarded as malevolent, but as capable of both destruction and aid.[42] One may drown in a river or lake, but one needs the water to live and to grow crops. One may be struck down by lightning, yet the lightning brings green to the land in the spring. And although the *naga* may take offense at human beings and their thoughtless encroachments on his sphere, he also may keep the sacred teachings in trust for a future generation and, as tradition has it, rise up, open his serpentine hood, and shelter the Buddha during his meditation—a role much like that of the serpentine beings in Native American tradition.

Of the "Quivira Indians," who were living in this sacred headwaters region in far greater concentration than whites currently are (it has been estimated that local population at the time of Coronado's military expedition was in the tens of thousands), we have little trace today. But these Caddoan-speaking peoples did form several later tribes, among whom are the Pawnee and the Wichita, to whose cosmology and metaphysics we still have some access. In any case, since the serpentine site dates to long before the sixteenth century, we are in fact reconstructing the meaning of a site from nearly a millennium ago, chiefly through reliance on the conservative tendency of all religious traditions and of the Pawnee in particular.[43]

Even though Native American traditions rely upon both individual and cyclic renewals that often correspond with a new ambience or landscape, one can discern within all of the tribal traditions great antiquity, not least because of the simplicity and purity of the symbolism they continue. One can see in the Algonquian *jossakid*, or shamanic medium, the continuation of a shamanic tradition that is found in Siberia, Australia, and elsewhere around the world, and that is of the greatest antiquity.[44] Likewise, among the astrological symbolism of the Pawnee, one sees also the continuation of traditions from great antiquity, and this is particularly true of the ceremonies and symbolisms of the Great Horned Serpent.

The holy men of the Skidi Pawnee, following visionary instructions, would build a sixty-foot-long serpent and a facsimile witch in a twenty-day-long ceremony, the serpentlike creature curving with its head toward the southeast, its forked tail to the northeast, its body curved around toward the west. The body was made of ashwood covered with grass, then clay, then painted; and the head was large enough for a man to crawl inside. The serpent's head had horns, or willow rods, protruding; both head and tail were forked. Later, to finish the ceremony, the tribesmen would carry the unpegged serpent and the witch down to a flowing creek, toward the southeast. After they laid the serpent near the bank, people would make offerings to it and request longevity and greatness for themselves or their children. Then the serpent and the witch would be put in the water and pegged, with the gifts, to the streambed inside a fence with a westward opening. Finally, the holy men would cause one another to fall into the water, signifying rebirth, and they would retire to a banquet.[45]

The horned serpent, in Pawnee as in Hopi tradition, was affiliated with holy springs and subterranean waters emerging into this world.[46] Water not only represents purification, but it is an indispensable physical element and the source of life. At the same time, the horned water spirit with its forked tail—a creature that reappears all across the Americas—manifests the reflection below of transcendent power. Like any power, then, the effects of the water spirit can be beneficent or malevolent.

This is why, when the Skidi Federation of the Pawnee built a sixty-foot serpent that was pegged to the base of the creek, they were in fact pegging down and controlling the serpentine reflection in the waters of the transcendent power above. The four horns of the water monster correspond to the four points of the cross or square within the circle that represents the center of tribal religion; but whereas the squared circle represents the harmony of heaven and earth, the writhing serpent with its forked head and tail corresponds to division, to the "waters below," to the chaos "beneath" earthly existence. Pegging the serpent down reinforces the cosmic order; the water purifies.

There is a cosmological significance to the Amerindian traditions that connects directional and stellar symbolism as well. The Great Horned Serpent of Lyons is aligned from northwest—the direction affiliated with lightning by the Pawnee—to southeast—the direction affiliated with the mysterious Red Star that controlled the coming of the animals. The Great Horned Serpent is also affiliated with the Black Star, through whom humans learn the secrets of the animals.[47] All of this suggests only the obvious: that the stars, the secrets of nature, and the directional spirits were all interwoven. The holy man understands the intricate tapestry of our cosmos in a much deeper way than the ordinary person; and his gnosis, combined with a proper way of living, determines his afterlife as well.

Now in Ojibway tradition, it is said that when one dies, one "travels" westward until faced with the temptation of a large fruit—in Ojibway tradition, a strawberry. If one succumbs to temptation, one is lost, but if one keeps going, there will appear a wavering bridge over the lower waters. This bridge is in fact a serpent, whose head is pointing to this side of the waters; one must cross it in order to reach the western paradise that was created by Nanabozhu, the demiurge represented in Ojibway mythology.[48] This serpentine monster represents the forces of the chaotic lower waters and appears in intitiation ritual maps for the esoteric Midé society as well; one must cross over the serpent, in order to reach paradise, and cannot return, for the way back is guarded by a great dog.

Above, a glyph signifying the serpentine or chthonic power; after Tomkins, Universal Sign Language of The Plains Indians, *1926. Below, a spirit-being recognized by the Winnebagos; drawing by Little Hill, a chief of that tribe. From Schoolcraft,* History of the Indian Tribes, *1854.*

In Menominee tradition, there are said to be four tiers beneath the earth, and that closest to the earth is the tier of the Horned Snake, Misikinu'bikuk, whose servant is a dog. The Horned Snakes are also called the Hairy Snakes and are relentlessly hunted by the Thunderbirds; a dreamer or visionary who sees a Horned Snake needs to break his fast and begin again, for the Misikinu'bikuk are an evil omen. Among the Menominee, the Horned Snake is seen as predominately destructive power. Among the Shoshone, the Horned Serpent reappears in the "Horned Water Buffalo" that lives in some lakes, an adaptation of the same symbolism.[49]

In any event, power remains power; and in those who are aware of it, it creates awe and dread. The Horned Snake represents this power. Shamans among the Algonquian are said to be in possession of some part of the Horned Snake, such as a scale, and to use an image or outline of the Horned Snake to work magic. Widespread among all the Algonquian-speaking tribes is the recognition that people kidnapped by the Horned Snakes become one of them, as is the recognition that ordinary weapons are useless against them. Among the Menominee a shaman is known as *kin'ubik-inaniwuk,* which means those men who have gotten their power from the Horned Serpents.[50]

At the same time, one finds the tradition that, beneath the earth, in the Waters Below, the Horned Snakes, like the *nagas* of Buddhist tradition, guard beneficent sacred treasure or medicine.[51] In Pawnee tradition, the chief spirit of the spiritual doctors was the Water Monster, or Great Horned Serpent, which took a man into the "animal lodge" in the Missouri River and showed him animal secrets and language.[52] One finds the Horned Snake affiliated with bodies of water, swamps, and certain kinds of hills, as well as with certain springs. Whatever the locale, the wise propitiate the Snakes with a small sacrifice in order to avoid calamity.

At this point we can begin to understand the cosmological significance of the Horned Snake more adequately. The Horned Snake—the symbolism of which is found all the way across North American Native traditions— embodies what we might call the subtle disequilibrium inherent in the cosmos; this power is the reflection of transcendent harmony, the secret of life itself. Disequilibrium must exist, for just as light against any material object causes a shadow, so too as the Divine separates itself from itself, in order to leave room for the cosmos, there is a disharmony created; it is the "residue" or inverse reflection in the lower waters of the harmony above.[53] The Horned Serpent represents the power inherent in life itself.

Thus we can begin to see the connection—which appears among virtually all of the Woodlands and Plains traditions—among the "divine Fools," the Sun, Fire, Lightning, and the Horned Serpents. For both the "contraries" (or in Sioux, *heyokas*, those who do everything backward) and the Horned Serpent represent "reversed" reflections of transcendent harmony. All the Plains traditions have "divine Fools": among the Omaha are the *hethuska;* among the Iowa and Ponca, the *helocka;* among the Kansa, the *helucka;* among the among the Dakota, the *heyoka;* and among the Pawnee are the "Children of the Sun," the *iruska.* These "contraries" do everything idiotically, or backward; that is their function within the tribe.

For instance, among the Pawnee, the *iruska,* or "Children of the Sun," were always painted black, their totem was the blackbird, and they always acted on backward commands as well. If their village were attacked, they would go on idiotically playing a wheel game until someone said, "Do not attack," and then they would attack the enemy by idiotically shooting arrows in the air, then running after them for retrieval.[54] Likewise, among the Arikara the *sakhu'nu,* or "Foolish Ones," were not allowed to marry or do the ordinary things of life; rather, they did everything in reverse. If they were asked to fight, they would not fight; if they were asked not to fight, they would fight. The story is told that the *sakhu'nu* were once outside an encampment and saw a peculiar red snake. "Let us not kill it," they said, and so they killed it. As a result, the encampment was veritably flooded with snakes rising up against them; people had to climb atop whatever they could, and many died.[55] Such a tale—even in this attenuated form—illustrates the connection between the unnatural (cosmic disequilibrium), the snakes, and the "contraries."

But this is not to say that the *iruska* or *heyoka* represent purely "negative" forces—quite the opposite, in fact. They embody the irruption into and the resolution of cosmic conflict in the human world: for the *heyoka* manifest directly into human society the perpetual conflict between the Thunderbird Powers above, of the west, and the Great Horned Serpents below. Only one who has witnessed the Thunder Beings of the west in a vision can be a *heyoka,* or "divine Fool." As Hehaka Sapa put it, those who have seen the Thunder Beings in a vision

have sacred power, and they share some of this with all the people, but they do it through funny actions. When a vision comes from the Thunder

Beings of the West, it comes with terror like a thunderstorm; but when the storm of vision has passed, the world is greener and happier; for whenever the truth of vision is upon the world, it is like a rain. The world, you see, is happier after the terror of the storm.[56]

What then is the connection between the Great Horned Serpent, the "divine Fools," and lightning, or fire? According to the Lakota, the *heyoka* are those who have seen the Thunderbirds in a vision, and because of this they are able to reach into boiling water with bare hands to take out pieces of boiled dog meat during the *heyoka* ceremony; they are able to predict stormy weather, and in some cases to control it; they have by way of vision "taken inside" the power of lightning or fire.[57] Among many Plains tribes, the "Children of the Sun" were directly affiliated with the fire-walking ceremony, or variants of it, showing their invulnerability to lightning or fire. In other words, the "contraries" embodied precisely the power that controlled or overcame the watery, serpentine powers below, that of the Thunder Beings, of the Sun, of Fire.[58]

About the *heyoka* Frithjof Schuon writes:

> The *heyoka* were men who, having been honored in a dream by the vision of the Thunderbirds, had thereby contracted the obligation, on the one hand, to humble themselves, and on the other, to dissimulate their consecration. Their case was similar, in certain respects, to that of the dervishes known by the name of the "people of blame" (*malamatiya*), who sought to attract the reprobation of the profane and the hypocritical, while realizing inwardly the most perfect spiritual sincerity. . . . The behavior of the *heyoka* amounts to an initiatory language, comprehensible only to sages, as well as being a sacrificial vocation, that of being a "walking dead man," and called upon to reëstablish inwardly the bridge between the world of matter and that of the spirit and immortality.[59]

The "divine Fools" make people laugh; they represent transcendent, even destructive powers harnessed within the tradition, and through their apparently foolish actions they restore equilibrium. By contrast, those who use power for selfish or evil purposes are witches, sorcerers, or "two-hearts" who in the end will pay.[60] In brief: One who contacts power has a responsibility to manifest it properly.

During some of the oldest Pawnee ceremonies, the holy men would keep their feet upon a model of the Great Horned Serpent beneath them, and it is said that from this "Water Monster" they would take their power to perform feats of magic, making corn sprout and grow tall in but a few moments, making cherries or plums ripen on the tree before one's eyes, or killing each other and then restoring each other to life again.[61] Within the traditional world of the Pawnee, the vital, mysterious power of the "Water Monster" was controlled by the holy men and used for universal benefit—their feet were upon it. But wherever the traditional unity and control of this power was disrupted, there arose the danger of misuse, of bad medicine.[62]

All of this symbolism is contained within a single glyph, a serpent lying on an angle across an axis. Above the serpent's head on the axis are three lines, signifying the three worlds beneath which the Great Horned Serpent exists. Below the serpent on the axis is "rooting," signifying the primal chaos beneath all manifestation. The Great Horned Serpent in a sense is life's vital power, a reflection of the transcendent power above. If this glyph were represented on an east-west axis, then the serpent in it would precisely correspond to the orientation of the Lyons Great Horned Serpent to the northwest.[63]

The Great Horned Serpent terraglyph in central Kansas, then, represents a whole nexus of symbolism. Located above the headwaters of the Little Arkansas River, it is found in a region rich with springs and, sometimes near them, sacred petroglyphs on the rock faces. The Great Horned Serpent marks the whole headwaters region, with all its sacred springs, and is in fact the sign of the spirit that lives there. Affiliated with its eternal enemies, the Thunder Beings, and with the "divine Fools" who have seen them, as with the lightning that is their sign, the Great Horned Serpent reveals the very powers of the cosmos itself, and so its symbolism creates both respect and dread.

In sum, the Great Horned Serpent, with its two horns and its forked tail, signifies the vital power of life itself in its dual aspect. On the one hand, this power, can make the corn grow, can make one invulnerable to fire, can make the dead live again, can heal the sick. On the other hand, this power, when used for egotistic or sorcerous purposes, destroys and lays waste, spreads death and destruction. In olden times, the tribal traditions controlled this power to the benefit of all beings; it showed the tribal peoples the secrets of the animals and plants, and they gave sacrifices to it. But when modern civilization destroys the traditions that allowed communal control of this dual power, the bonds once holding the world together are sundered, more individualistic tendencies prevail, and humanity's central place in the cosmic cycle is abandoned.

In a sense an emblem of life on earth, the Great Horned Serpent represents the eternal, constant dance between the powers above and the powers below, and it reveals to us the two paths we each face—on the one hand the path of evil, of destruction, of individualism, greed, anger, and folly; and on the other hand, the path of universal benefit, of generosity, compassion, and wisdom that controls. Now, as always, the choice is before us.

3

THE STONE MAN

As you travel west through Kansas, the landscape grows more open, the horizon widens, the golden brown hills roll on and on with ever-fewer signs of modern civilization. It is as though you were traveling out of modern civilization; here the open rangeland seems little changed from what it must have looked like centuries ago, when the buffalo came in great herds across it. The landscape itself is timeless; and as you travel to the highest place in it, you find—as always in this prairie land—that you know you are on the highest place only when you're there, as a shock or a revelation, for all around, the horizon is ringed by rolling brown hills. On this rock-strewn bluff, where the wind blows in from the north, you can see in every direction; here, in this sacred place, you are at the heart of the world, and spread out below you is the Stone Man.

The Stone Man is an outline of a giant in small stones set relatively deep in the earth, some of which have even been completely covered by earth, indicating the outline's antiquity. Laid out on the slightly eastward incline of the bluff's wide, flat plateau, the Man is placed on a west-east axis, with the plateau extending north and south, although especially northward. The

Stone Man's head-and-body axis is more west-southwest to east-northeast, rather than clearly east-west, which suggests that the Man embodies the totality of directional symbolism, of which we will say more shortly. This sacred site is unique to the southern Plains.

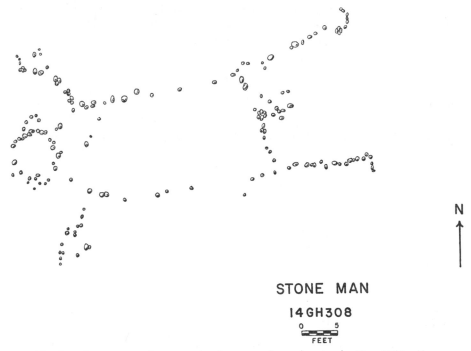

N
↑

STONE MAN
14GH308
0 — 5
FEET

The Penokee Man, a figure made of stones; after a drawing by Tom Witte, Kansas State Historical Society.

Standing at the site, atop this high bluff, with the serpentine river to the south, strong winds blowing across the plateau to the north, and below, in the distance, the foliage marking springs and creeks, one can see the Stone Man's remaining stones. Many of the stones are missing now. It has been well over a century since the last of the original people came here to visit this site. The rancher whose family has owned the land since the late nineteenth century tells you that his great-grandparents burned tipi poles to keep warm. But that was the year the last buffalo herd was killed, and the tribes did not return again to the ancient campsites to the west of this Stone Man. Standing here on a cool autumn afternoon in the bright sunshine, you wonder what the Stone Man meant to the tribal peoples.

To the south, on the southern-facing bluff over the Solomon River, there are still stone cairns. Once there were countless such cairns, but the ranchers took them away to build foundations and walls, and now only these few are left, to the south-southwest of the Stone Man. If one were to draw a line from the Stone Man to the remaining cairns, one would mark the point at which Orion, the Great Hunter—also known as the Giant in many religious traditions—appears in early spring. As a Pawnee star map more than three hundred years old and painted on buckskin reveals, the Pawnee and their ancestors and relatives possessed a very specific and accurate knowledge of the night sky, and in particular of Orion and the Milky Way. In this map, found in a sacred bundle, Orion is shown precisely in this point at early spring on the south-southwest of the horizon.[64] Perhaps there are correspondences among spring, when the world turns green and vital again, the Great Hunter, Orion, and the Stone Man, with his once-prominent *virilia*.

The Stone Man is made of small stones more than a handsbreadth in size, and he lies with his arms upraised. He has pronounced ears, and the accounts that survive of him, from the nineteenth century, say that he originally had a "heart line" stretching from his mouth down to his heart. He had male genitalia. Today, one can hardly see the arms, nothing of the heart line, and little of the genitalia. But if we take the symbolic significance of just the characteristics mentioned, we will be able to understand what the Stone Man really means.

Above all, we need to recognize the significance of stone itself in Amerindian traditions and indeed universally among traditional religions. Stone signifies the *prima materia;* the primordial coalescing of the primal Substance underlying all Creation. Hence, stones are considered to contain the secret of Creation itself, in a certain sense; and therefore just as at the center of Islam is the Qaaba, or sacred stone of Mecca, and just as at the center of Iroquois tradition was the sacred stone of the nation, so too many individual tribesmen and women have sacred stones as well. It is true in a certain sense that all Creation is sacred; but there are certain places—and certain stones—in which that sacredness "coalesces."

It is said that the secret of alchemy is *solve et coagula,* or "dissolve and coalesce," and without doubt this is at the center of the mystery of the Stone Man as well. For to understand the significance of the Stone Man, as of any visionary sacred site, one must be able to enter into what Henry Corbin calls the "imaginal world," the archetypal world of which this world, and especially this sacred site, is a reflection. The physical must "dissolve" to reveal the "coagulated" spiritual or archetypal reality. This is the heart of the Stone Man, which was without doubt a visionary place, a site to which one would travel for fasting and spiritual revelation.

Everything about this site is conducive to entering that imaginal symbolic world. Indeed, in universal Amerindian pictographic or symbolic language, a figure of a man with a line from the heart to the mouth signified inspiration. The heart signifies the center of the being; the line from the head to the heart denotes the complete integration of spiritual truth into the being or spiritual revelation. The arms upraised universally indicate man in a state of petition to Divine power; the large ears of the Stone Man connote spiritual hearing or receptivity to the Divine. The genitals indicate virility, vitality, the power of life itself, coming to life in the spring.

It should be noted, however, that in form what we have been calling the Stone Man actually is the figure of a giant, with a long torso and short legs. Many of the tribal traditions speak of a race of giants that once existed on earth but that eventually rebelled against the Creator and were wiped out by a great flood, to be replaced by human beings. Wichita tradition in particular speaks of giants whose torsos grew far too large for their legs, who grew destructive, and who had to be destroyed by a flood.[65] There is a direct connection here not only with other religious traditions, including the Christian, Hindu, Buddhist, Norse, and Judaic, but with the doctrines of a creator-demiurge, and of a human being as microcosmos.[66]

But first we need to note, briefly, the connection between the demiurge-creator and giants. Among Indo-European traditions—from Celtic and Norse to Hindu and Buddhist—and in esoteric Judeo-Christian and Islamic traditions as well, a race of giants is said to have existed in an earlier age and to have become irreligious and destructive. These giants correspond to the "fallen angels" of Christian tradition; and in all these traditions, they were said to have been contained by higher powers.[67] But to this day, in Europe and Asia, as in America, there are places of great antiquity, in particular stones, that are affiliated with the giants. These giants are in folklore or esoteric tradition universally seen as belonging to an earlier time cycle than our own, and as instinct with the very power of demiurgic creation itself; the giants, it is said, taught human beings many secrets.

In Blackfoot tradition, it is said that the demiurge, called Old Man, made all things, and all birds, animals, plants, and people understood him, just as he understood them, having made them. He traveled from south to north, it is said, and on his way lay down, leaving his imprint in stones on a high knoll.[68] Among the Pawnee, there is a wonderful man by the name of Pahukatawa, who was killed by the Sioux but was resurrected by the spirits of the heavens, the birds, and the animals. Pahukatawa gives the Pawnee the secrets of the earth; it is he who tells tribesmen how to avoid or eliminate diseases, how to find the buffalo, and when the enemy is attacking. After his death, he was affiliated with a star in the northwest, and it is said that he offers to humans the secrets of the animal spirits.[69]

In these two myths we have reversals of the same fundamental truth: in the Blackfoot myth, we have the demiurge creating the natural world; in the Pawnee myth, we have man resurrected by virtue of the spirits of the natural world. The two myths are like mirror images of each other; in the first we see how man and the spirits of nature are of one patrimony; in the second, we see how those spirits not only came from man but help him to live, in a sense returning him to true spiritual life. In Christian terms, we might well say that the Old Man corresponds to Adamic man, conceived of in spiritual terms as Adam Kadmon, or the Great Man; and Pahukatawa corresponds to Christic man, man redeemed from death and resurrected, man who knows the secret truth within creation.

Both myths reveal truths about the Stone Man stretched out before us on this high knoll. These too are "giant stones" like those found in northern Europe to this day; it is not that they are large stones but that they remind us of the "age of the giants," of the titanic power that infills all of Creation. Simultaneously, they reveal to us how nature in her entirety is like a Great Man, a macro-anthropos, how the birds, the plants, the animals, the earth, the very stones themselves bespeak the same transcendent power that created man; and how man in turn is microcosm, how within him, by virtue of the divine inspiration signified by the heart line, are the secret powers, the languages, the spiritual archetypes of all Creation.

In many Amerindian traditions, it is said that people can by revelation come to know the language of spirits, the language of animals, the language of birds, the language of plants, the language of stones. Indeed, there is a sense in which the pictographs or glyphic symbols that appear on rocks, and sometimes on other surfaces across the Americas, give us insight into and manifest "the language of the spirits." A glyph represents a nexus of symbolism; it can embody a whole range of significances at once, as is the case with the Stone Man. This is in a way what is meant by "language of the spirits": one understands in a nonlinear, nonsuccessive, multidimensional way an *imaginal*, or archetypal, reality.

The holy man is one who is at home in this imaginal or archetypal reality; anything that he encounters can reveal its symbolic or archetypal truth, which is relatively independent of time and space. A vision can reveal itself through anything; a spirit may send a messenger, may reveal its message through a sign, through something seen or heard, or in a spoken communication revealed in what in Lakota is called *hanbloglaka*, or "visionary language." Essentially, the visionary language is the revelation of the symbolic or archetypal truth at the heart of things. This visionary language is understood by the holy man, for whom the spirit world is familiar.[70]

A sacred site like this one—the Stone Man—represents an "opening" from the physical world to the archetypal or spirit world and therefore is itself in a certain sense a manifestation of visionary language, even as it is a place conducive to a revelation in that language. The Stone Man himself—with his upraised arms, with his listening ears, with his heart line, with his nakedness—is primordial man, man transmuted, man open to the visionary world. He is made of rocks, the fundament of Creation, its coagulated Substance; and yet he is also visionary Reality, not at all merely a physical monument but an entry point into the imaginal or spirit world.

Man is exiled on earth from his spiritual, paradisal home; he, and all of nature, is exiled into physical manifestation from the freedom and relative eternity of the archetypal or imaginal realm of the "far North." We suffer, and we die. Yet this exile is also our gift, for what we do on this earth where we are grounded creates our state in the afterlife.

This is the secret of the Stone Man: what we do here on earth creates our afterlife. To moderns, some tribal practices seem strangely materialistic, as for instance when a man goes out and fasts in order to win at war or to win a woman in love. But we need to understand that the physical world reflects the archetypal realm, and that it is not separate from the transcendent, spiritual origin of both. Every action in this world is also an action in the archetypal world: to fall in love or to take an enemy in war is also to establish a relationship with that individual in the next world.[71] What is more, if we attain a certain degree of gnosis in this world, that will be our degree in the next; for what separates this world and the next is the absence of materiality's opaqueness or limitation.

The Stone Man lies before us, stretched out upon the earth, a reminder of the visionary world borne within nature always. A shadow passes: an eagle is circling to the west. We stand here on this high knoll and look at the horizon's ring as the sun lights the western sky with red and orange. Everything around us is transmuted into gold by the sun's setting. There is little sign of modern civilization here, but the traditions are nonetheless gone; the tribes have long since gone. And yet standing here on this plateau, the veil between this world and the next seems more translucent; standing here beside this Stone Man, in whom is joined above and below, sky and rock, the visionary world can still open. Could it ever really be otherwise?

4

THE GREAT LODGE
AS MICROCOSMOS

Among all the Native American tribes, there is some form of microcosmic Great Lodge, whether it be an Iroquois, Ojibway, Delaware, Pueblo, Hopi, Cheyenne, Pawnee, or Sioux variation. Naturally, there are as many permutations of the Great Lodge as there are cultural and geographic variations, but underlying these is a single cosmological perspective. Each of the Native American religiocultural groups reveals in its image of the Great Lodge different aspects of the same cosmological understanding.

This is not to say that there are not fundamental differences among the Native American religious traditions, only to say that these religious traditions reflect an underlying consensus. In the same way, one can more generally see fundamental patterns among all the world's religious traditions. The spiritual quest of mankind seems everywhere—in essential ways—to be the same. Of course one cannot deny the richness and diversity of the world's religious traditions, nor of the North American native religious traditions: indeed, in this variance and adaptability is their resilient strength.

But if one cannot accept as well that the world's religious traditions all reflect different aspects of the same essential spiritual truths, one would be denying spiritual truth itself, in the kind of inversion inherent in euhemerism.

Unfortunately, the modern university, for example, tends to compartmentalize religious traditions, believing that the pursuit of knowledge is best served by progressive fragmentation or particularization of our understanding. The divisions between anthropology and archaeology and religious studies and the history of art seem to assume that each of these is a separate box into which one can shove the authentic traditions that are our universal inheritance as human beings. Yet can anyone seriously argue that these "separate" disciplines are unrelated and that they are not studying essentially the same things?

We must keep in mind that in spiritual terms modern civilization is crippled and needs to reconstruct, from the fragments of traditions we today possess, something of the wholeness inherent in a traditional culture. To do this, we may at times turn to different religious traditions, in order that these can illuminate for us our own tradition. There is in this an artificiality: to understand Amerindian traditions by reference to Persian Sufi spirituality is at first glance outré. But ours are abnormal times, and in compensation for our spiritual poverty, we do have access (albeit in an attenuated way) to the larger whole of the world's religious traditions. No tradition is untouched by the erosions of our day, but perhaps by putting together the pieces we have, we can reconstruct something of the original wholeness, if we are also inspired by the spirit that informs those parts.

So it is with the Great Lodge. When we look at each of the tribal traditions and see how they correspond, we find at those nexus points not just felicitous connections but a fundamentally unified cosmological understanding manifesting in particular ritual forms across geographical areas. This unity is especially evident when we consider the general significance of the Great Lodge in terms of spiritual geography.

As one travels north in America, one tends to find a more individualized spirituality, which manifests in the shamanic traditions of the Algonquin, for instance; whereas as one travels south, one finds an ever more centralized or communal spirituality, as seen in the vast ceremonial centers of the Aztec, the Maya, and even of southeastern American tribes like the Hopi or the Zuñi, whose spirituality is in some ways more communal than that of, say, the Shoshone, the Ojibway, or the Menominee.[72] In the north one tends find more temporary lodges; in the south one finds more permanent lodges and more communal, or agrarian-based, ceremonial traditions.

More important than geographical differences, however, is the cosmological unity that underlies the different traditions, in particular the element of directional symbolism and its meaning in spiritual geography. In any spiritual tradition, directional symbolism does not necessarily refer merely to spatial coordinates. Rather, the Great Lodge is a representation of a visionary cosmos, and the spiritual vision that informs it takes absolute precedence over our ordinary views of "history" or "spatiality."

Essentially, the term *visionary directional symbolism* means that directionality is conceived not in physical but in symbolic and cosmological terms. In symbolic terms, east means potentiality and is affiliated with the Upper Waters, the Ocean of Informal, or supraindividual, Possibility; west, on the other hand, means realized potential, the Lower Waters, the Ocean of Formal, or individual, Possibility. East, or dawn, therefore corresponds to the supraindividual state and its translation into this world; west, or sunset, on the other hand, corresponds to the day's fruition, to reaping the fruits of our actions. This is why the west is in so many traditions—including the native North American—the direction of Paradise.

According to Lakota Sioux tradition, as discussed earlier, the east-west axis is the "blue or black road," which is the road of error and destruction, of sensuality and ignorance, while the south-north axis is the "red road," the "straight and narrow path."[73] But how can this symbolism correspond with the virtually universal Native American tradition of facing a Great Lodge and other sacred sites along an east-west axis, particularly if west is affiliated with the paradisal? Our answer is found in a visionary treatise written by Shamsuddin Muhammad Lahiji, in his Persian commentary on the *Rose Garden of the Mystery* (*Gulshan-i Raz*) by Mahmud Shabistari, translated by Henry Corbin.

In Persian visionary theosophy, a tradition speaks of the two cities of Jabalqa in the east and Jabarsa in the west. According to this tradition, the eastern city of Jabalqa is the interworld midway between the suprasensible world and the physical realm; spirits "descend" into existence from the translucent purity of the eastern city. The western city of Jabarsa, conversely, is the interworld in which spirits dwell when they have left the earthly realm; there exist the Forms of all completed Works or earthly actions, and from this western city spirits "ascend." According to the Muslim Shaikh Muhyiddin

Ibn Arabi, the city of the east is the mystery of the Futurable, while the city of the west is the mystery of the Irreversible, because from the east earthly life is "ahead," while from the West, earthly life is "behind" and "irreversible."[74]

This elaboration from Persian visionary theosophy helps us to understand the symbolism of east and west in human terms, but it does not yet explain how it is that the east-west axis can at once symbolize the spiritual path of the being, and yet also be the road to destruction. The answer to this conundrum comes from the recognition that visionary directional symbolism does not correspond to spatiality and can possess multiple, even directly conflicting, meanings, for the east-west axis, in traditional symbolism, corresponds to, and in a real sense is a transposition of, north-south axial symbolism. As Henry Corbin puts it, "The *Orient-origin,* which *orients* and magnetizes the [spiritual] return and ascent, is the celestial pole, the cosmic North."[75]

We are oriented not by the east but by the Pole of the cosmos, which is in the north. This means that the symbolism of north and east, south and west each correspond. North is the direction of purity; it is the direction from which the spirits come, and the Origin or Axis of the worlds; it corresponds to the east. South, on the other hand, is the direction of the ancestors, of warmth, of fruition of deeds, and corresponds to the west in these respects. Hence the Sioux, the Ojibway, the Cheyenne, and many other tribes speak at times of the south and at times of the west as the "place" where the dead go.

Here too lies the key to the meaning of the Milky Way as the celestial "path of the dead." For the Milky Way appears to us as oriented semicardinally, from southwest to northeast. This path, practically speaking, conjoins the symbolism of south and west on the one hand, and north and east on the other. One "travels" northward to the celestial Paradise at the Axis of the world; this is the meaning of the "northern Paradise" found in many tribal traditions.

Such cosmological symbolism is particularly well represented in the largest of these lodges, those of the Creeks. The Great Lodges of the Creeks, like those of the Cherokee, were conical circular buildings, but the Creek domes were capable of holding several hundred people within them and included much of ritual significance. During Creek Great Lodge or council house ceremonies, there would be a spiral of cane grass laid out around the central pillar, on which flames would spontaneously arise. As long as the grass burned, the meeting would continue. The flames signified the course of the sun at night, which reminds us of the symbolism of the "sun at midnight" in the Greco-Roman mystery tradition.[76]

The daily council work of the chiefs or warriors, however, was done in a longhouse that as one of four longhouses formed the perimeter of the village square. This other council house was split in two; on one lengthwise side was deposited all the sacred things of the tribe, including the great pipe, or calumet, a white eagle's tail displayed like a fan and attached to a staff, and sacred bundles. On the other side—the front—the chiefs, warriors, and others met to deliberate. This arrangement meant that the tribal decisions were permeated with the sacred influence of the holy icons on the other side of the same building.

In both the rotunda, or great circular council house, and in this longhouse, the inhabitants were divided into three orders, corresponding to the priestly, warrior, and common classes. This triune division corresponds, again, to the "three worlds" of celestial, subtle, and terrestrial reality, as does the triune division of the entire village center into circular rotunda, tetragonally placed longhouses, and large village square, with its three poles. One is not surprised to find that the longhouses are totemically decorated, for it is here that the "upper," ceremonial, celestial world and the "lower," physical world meet; it is here that the subtle realm manifests in all its symbolic richness.

Among the Cheyenne, there was a ceremony called the Massaum, a name said to derive from *massa'ne*, meaning "foolish," and connecting the Massaum Lodge ceremony to the "Contraries." The Massaum Lodge ceremony is said to have been revealed "beneath the earth" in "underground lodges," which suggests to us again the rebirth symbolism entailed in, for example, the Hopi kiva and emergence myths. Emerging from below to above signals a change of state, a spiritual ascent or a rebirth.

The Massaum Lodge is located within a larger iconoscape: to the north is the Grass Buffalo Lodge, in the northeast is the Gray Wolf Lodge, and in the west is the Fox Lodge. There are essentially two trails around this circular spiritual landscape: the Gray Wolf Trail begins in the north and travels around the Massaum Lodge in the center and then follows the sun south and west, circling the four directions, ending before the east-facing Massaum Lodge again. The Fox Trail begins in the west, travels eastward, and then circles in the same direction as the Gray Wolf Trail, save that at each of the cardinal points it doubles back, and in the northeast quadrant it doubles back several times. To follow these trails is to "circle the square" of the four directions, to join heaven and earth.

Note the celestial symbolism here. The Fox Trail begins in the west, the direction of the setting sun, of the day's deeds made manifest; the Gray Wolf trail begins in the north, the polar direction, the Axis of the worlds. But both trails end in the east; symbolically, both north and west have been assimilated into the east and into its orienting significance as dawn, as the beginning of a new spiritual day. The Fox Trail might be said to correspond with the Osirian mysteries of Egyptian tradition, while the Gray Wolf Trail would correspond to the Mysteries of Ra.[77] To follow the trails is to become a "new man," to be reborn at the eastern "opening" of the primordial cosmos.

It is not surprising, given the predominance of the north in this spiritual landscape in which the Massaum Lodge exists, that within the lodge not north but south should prevail. The lodge itself has an eastern entrance, of course, and near the entrance is the fire, just as the sun rises to the east. In the center is the pole; to the west is the painted buffalo skull, signifying spiritual fruition. Above the skull, at about a man's height, a spiritual guardian with buffalo horns and eagle-talon feet is painted on the wall. But the box elder's spiritual bundle, the rattles, the pipe—as well as all the important dignitaries—sit to the south of the center. Only the yellow wolf skin, on which is painted the sign of lightning, is to the north of center, in the northwest. This is as it should be—for in relation to the spiritual Axis in the north, man is always situated in the south, the direction affiliated with the ancestors in many traditions.[78]

As with the Cheyenne Massaum Lodge, so one finds with the Pawnee Deer Dance Lodge: one enters from the east and circumnavigates from east to south to west to north, reflecting the circumpolar movement of the stars. This symbolism is made overt in the arrangement of those seated within the Deer Dance Lodge, for youths are seated in the southeast, mature men in the southwest, older men in the northwest, and the elderly in the north or northeast. The east is affiliated with red and the north with black; one finds that these colors are very often linked in ceremonial painting, reinforcing once again the ultimate unity of the beginning and the end of a cycle, birth and death, east and north. North is affiliated with black because it represents transcendence, the inconceivable.

The same elemental symbolism is represented in any of the Great Lodges, including those of the Midéwiwin of the Ojibway: here too the opening is to the east and the altar is to the west; here too there is a fire and axial symbolism. But in the Midéwiwin ceremonial lodge, the symbolism of spiritual rebirth is made explicit, for inside the lodge take place the initiation ceremonies depicted on birchbark scrolls. An infant has a lodge built for it, and inside the lodge not only the baptism of the particular child takes place but the symbolic dying and rebirth of each of the participants in the ceremony, who not only expectorate the evil within them but are "struck" by Midé seashells, fall, and rise again.[79]

Here too, in the Midé lodge, the microcosmic symbolism is made clear: the intitiate enters from the east, passes through the four initiatory grades, and overcomes the Great Serpent at the western end. In the center of the lodge is the great drum, which signifies the pulse of life itself, and the drumstick signifies the great Tree of Life.[80] To reach the fourth level of Midé is by no means commonplace, but it represents the complete initiatory cycle, taking place within the cruciform directional symbolism, and within the sacred lodge that represents the whole cosmos.

The microcosmos symbolized within the Great Lodge, as a sacred place in which the mysteries can be performed and in which the elemental truths of our existence become clear, can be seen also in the lodge used for the inipi, or purification ceremony, of the Sioux. The lodge, like the purification lodges of all tribes, manifests the most elemental symbolism: it is constructed of willow trees, which die each autumn and are reborn each spring; inside, one has the heated rocks, the water; outside, one has the "eternal fire," and the wind. Inside, one is in darkness; outside is the light. The inipi is often performed in the winter, for it is in winter that we are in darkness, in winter that we are purified, reborn, drawn closer to the spirit world.[81] To leave the purification lodge is virtually to be liberated from the terrestrial world.

To read the spiritual landscape, to read the universal symbolism in any particular manifestation of the Great Lodge, requires a necessary degree of intellectual and imaginal illumination. This illumination is not "intellectual" in the limited, ratiocinative sense of the word; it is the illumination of the buddhi in Hindu terms, the penetrating, inclusive, transcendent vision of the "spotted eagle" in Prairie traditions. To truly enter into the significance of the Great Lodge—of the visionary landscape that it signifies—is to enter into a cosmos made transparent, in which all that surrounds us *orients* us toward the Divine.

To pass through the Great Lodge is to be reborn: it is to be illuminated by the Divine, because the lodge is an imaginal manifestation to us of our place in the cosmos as a whole. It is true that in historical times, under the erosive pressures of the whites' religious persecution—even as early as the mid nineteenth century—the orally and pictorially or symbolically transmitted traditions of many tribes were breaking down. Those traditions were perhaps even nearing the end of this transmissive cycle, for all that has happened in our declining age is destined. But the spiritual landscape and cosmological symbolism that the lodge bodies forth nonetheless always remains. Our physical world is in constant flux and must pass away, but that of which it is a reflection, and that for which we are destined, cannot pass away; it is our celestial Origin.

Initiation and Its Inversions

In all traditional religions one finds spiritual initiation, and the Native American traditions are no exception. Initiation, of course, presupposes a transmission and a lineage, a tradition of initiator and disciple that can be traced back through time to the original illumination. Such lineages are found in Islam, Buddhism, Hinduism, and Judaism, at least within the esoteric centers of these traditions. And one reason that Western Christians often have difficulty grasping the nature of other religious traditions is precisely the absence of this kind of master-disciple initiatory transmission.[82] The Native American religious traditions, although they do not stem from a single spiritual revealer like the Buddha, nonetheless include spiritual initiation. Initiation amounts ultimately to guaranteeing the authenticity of one's spiritual experience and to protecting one from spiritual error, the most destructive of which is sorcery, or inverted initiation.

Of course, the very term "spiritual initiation" has been subject to many interpretations: some still insist that initiation is nothing more than ritualized entry into a tribal community, while others seem to believe that initiation confers a spiritual experience. But if we define *initiation* as the transmitted opening of a spiritual possibility—or, more exactly, virtuality—within a human being, then initiation must be understood as representing far more than merely entry into some human community. This is not to say that one is actually "conferring" anything more than the possibility of realizing a certain station of being above ordinary human states of being.

Initiation guarantees the authenticity of one's spiritual experience in two central ways. *Before* one seeks, a holy man—the tradition—confers the spiritual means, or symbolic parameters. *After* one's experience, one shares one's vision or other experience with a human being who has deeper spiritual experience and who can acknowledge that a given insight or vision was not merely delusion. The modern world tends to denigrate tradition—the transmission of the means through which authentic spiritual experience may be realized.

In Native American traditions, as elsewhere, initiation may take a wide range of forms, but in principle initiation always entails guaranteeing spiritual experience as authentic. The holy man may prepare the young initiate and protect him from destructive or deluding powers, through a special kind of continuing contact during the seeking; or the holy men of a tribe together may offer such protection; or the tribal community and all the ancestors, spirits, and higher powers who guard it may protect the seeker. But in all cases, there is a collective spiritual protection and guidance that prevents the seeker from falling into evil states—so much as this protection is possible.

The seeker, after all, is ultimately on his own. When one is granted a spiritual gift like a vision one is alone, except in extraordinary revelations—as when White Buffalo Woman came to the Sioux. The community provides support, a place for spiritual practice, and the teachings that lead one to spiritual illumination—but an individual still is ultimately responsible for his own spirituality, for his own fate. This is evident when one is alone in virgin nature, fasting and lamenting one's human frailties, seeking divine illumination. The tribe supports the seeker, whose vision in turn nourishes and supports the tribal spirituality.

But despite the best intentions and the purest of traditional transmissions—even in an era relatively unpolluted by modernity—there still exists at least the possibility of a spiritual seeker not only failing in his quest but contacting dark or destructive powers. If one can ascend into the light, one can also sink into the darkness. What is more, once this kind of fall or spiritual perversion takes place within an initiative transmission, an inverted lineage of sorcery, or antispirituality, can be established as soon as one passes this sorcerous knowledge on.

Such inverted lineages are said to exist within the Christian world; indeed, there is increasing evidence of the black or dark path gaining adherents in modernity.[83] Sorcery and an inverted initiatory tradition, however, can only exist on the residue of an authentic tradition, for sorcery and black magic feed on the power that was controlled and used for beneficent spiritual purposes when within a tradition. One finds among the Ojibway the initiatory tradition of the Midéwiwin Lodge, with its birch scrolls marking the initiatory degrees through which the spiritual seeker passes; but one also finds among the Ojibway an inverted or dark cult, a Midé sorcerous transmission of "bearwalking" that entails killing or harming other people for egotistic ends.[84] Likewise among the Navaho there is a widespread "underground" fear of witches and sorcerers, which has grown exponentially as modernity has eroded and destroyed traditional spirituality, which otherwise protects against the inversion of the sacred.[85]

Among these inverted or sorcerous cults—existing on the residue or periphery of any tradition, including Christianity—there is a dark price to be paid for entry, just as there is traditionally a high price for legitimate initiation. Often it is said that one must offer up a relative or friend to be killed; this kind of betrayal makes one responsible for the death and links one indissolubly with the sorcerous lodge.[86] Always sorcery represents an illegitimate use of power for self-aggrandizement, and so the sorcerous cult—although it may appear to have some semblance of inverted unity— is ultimately a "coalescing" of fragmentation and destruction. It destroys community in all possible senses.

Of course, differentiation must be made between white misinterpretations of aboriginal religious traditions and actual sorcery. Unfortunately, many nineteenth- and early twentieth-century writers on Native American traditions regarded every aspect of Amerindian religion to be nothing more than sorcery or nonsense. Although that kind of ignorant dismissal of authentic traditional religious traditions has largely diminished, there is nonetheless a clear distinction to be made between authentic spiritual traditions and their inversions. Sorcery is illegitimately concerned with effects and power in this world, while authentic spiritual traditions—Native American, Judeo-Christian, Hindu, Muslim, and Buddhist—reveal the path to spiritual realization.

In earlier times, magical contests might take place between holy men who would hold lighthearted "battles" showing their prowess in performing certain miracles. But those contests were merely peripheral to the spiritual path of which they were an incidental manifestation. Modern times, however, have made the spiritual path much more difficult, and such benign contests are for the most part no longer held.[87] Today these benign or beneficent powers have waned. This kind of change results in large part from the nature of our era as a whole. Modern society steadfastly refuses to acknowledge the transcendent origin and meaning of existence, limiting itself to material and submaterial phenomena. This ignorance of all that exists beyond the physical—above and below—means in practice that we have cut ourselves off from the Divine and opened ourselves to the infernal.

As René Guénon lucidly observed, not quite midway through the twentieth century, the modern era has been marked essentially by an antitraditional movement, one that opposes or undermines the spiritual in every possible way.[88] Religion is denigrated in countless ways, while traditions are mocked and obliterated. In such a climate, one should not be surprised that there exists also sorcery, for sorcery is but the dark or inverted "residue" of traditional sciences, sciences turned toward egotistic and destructive ends. In a sense, one could say that the whole of modernity—technology in particular—represents a kind of sorcery, a pact with dark powers for which one pays with one's soul.

One can hardly expect, in an ambience like that created by the modern world, to find anything other than the kind of spiritual occlusion visible everywhere modernity has been able to reach. But despite this ambience, which spawns sorcerous, individualistic, destructive cults like those found in the "residues" of quasi-Asian groups that have appeared in the West— antitraditional cults generally focused around a single, rather monstrous leader—traditional spirituality is by no means gone.

We are certainly beset on all sides by forces intent on making us ignore our spiritual heritage and turning either toward the plundering of the earth or, worse, toward sorcerous evil and spiritual destruction. But authentic spiritual teachers are still to be found, and there are still sacred traditions that will protect and guide the spiritual seeker. Every tradition preserves a spiritual ambience more or less free from the pollutions of our age, in which one may practice. There can be no doubt that those who succumb to the lures or the pressures of materialism on the one hand, or far worse, to sorcery on the other, will reap what they sow. Likewise, those who follow an authentic spiritual path will find their rewards—for the greater the dangers one faces, and the greater the struggle, the greater the blessings.[89]

It is necessary in the present day to understand that spiritual truth is not found by chasing after magical effects and power as depicted in certain quasi-novelistic books of the late twentieth century that in fact reveal, not native traditional spirituality but mere sorcery and quasi-shamanic cults. Rather, spiritual truth is found in humility, in bending down before the majesty of one's own spiritual tradition and asking for guidance. Native Americans find this in their own spiritual traditions; Christians can find the truth within Christianity; Buddhists within Buddhism; Muslims within Islam; Hindus within Hinduism; Jews within Judaism. For if one enters sincerely into the heart of one's own tradition, the mysteries of existence will be made known; one will have entered into a transmuted world illumined by spiritual truth, entry into which is marked by authentic spiritual initiation, the bestowal of spiritual guidance and protection. This is a gift beyond price or imagination; it is the justification and the meaning of our existence.

PART III
SPIRITUAL LANDSCAPE

Introduction

The first European explorers saw the Americas as a threatening wilderness, full of adversity, a grim place to be overcome, its peoples "savages" to be killed like beasts. One can see this attitude still, and highlighted, in the gray, sober, stark remains of a settler's Plains farmhouse. The farmhouse, now ruined, was built upon a foundation made of the sacred stones from a nearby sacred site once dotted with symbolic rock mounds, or cairns. For that Plains farmer, whose family has now abandoned the homestead, this was a harsh land, to be struggled against. But for the Native Americans whose stones his house was built upon, this was visionary ground, one of the most sacred places in the Plains. We need to recognize such places, whatever our tradition.

Of course, that the stones were used to build the foundations of the homestead house, the barn, and the outbuildings indicates a continuity of sorts between Native American and white peoples. And if one talks to a second-, third-, or fourth-generation farmer or rancher around here, one will find that beneath the talk about the miserable market or about the decadence of modern urban life, there is a deep and abiding love for the land to which he or she was born. There will probably still be some hint of that earlier hatred for the Indians, but the Indians are gone now, for the most part, and so are regarded in a slightly different light than once they were.

For those who live on the land, the wisdom of the past soaks into them despite themselves; the past inhabits the present, symbolized by those sacred stones cemented into the foundation of that gray, decaying homestead. You cannot live in a place for generations and not let it seep into your bones, reform your soul, become deeply a part of you. The land itself absorbs us; its generous spirit embraces us, even with our arrogant ways, even with our taking up of the sacred stones to make a rock wall and a foundation for a profane house, because the land can wait. It knows that that house is transient too, that for all our belief in our own destiny, in the absurdities we vaunt as "progress," the buildings and walls will crumble, the people will move on.

How assured we moderns are of our own authority and eternity! To ourselves we have granted the right to do whatever we want to the land and the waters and the air. But the land, the waters, the winds, and the sun will far outlast roads and cities and machines. The landscape can be covered over, gouged out, poisoned, but its spiritual power remains, and in the end it will absorb and convert us as surely as the sun shall rise again. We can kill the buffalo, but their spirit remains on the great horizon's rim; they will thunder by in great herds long after our fences are gone and our grand illusions of owning the earth have evaporated like the fog they are. The land we see is a spiritual landscape, and to that landscape we now turn.

1
LANGUAGE of the EARTH, LANGUAGE of the Sky

In Polynesian tradition, there is an entire science of "reading" the ocean and the sky. Indeed, the lives of these ocean-going peoples depend upon knowledge of their position, of approaching storms, of approaching land, of many subtler things—all knowledge given them not just "empirically," but as signs and as part of what may be called an oceanic language. This language is a divine gift; it is indivisibly linked with the blessings and the wisdom of their deities.[90] The Americas, of course, reverse this situation of tiny islands amid a vast ocean—for the Americas are vast stretches of land. Nonetheless, just as the Polynesians know the ocean and its moods and "tastes," so too the Native Americans living in the wildernesses of the Americas know the languages of earth and sky.

The word *language* implies meaning. The phrase "language of earth and sky" does not refer merely to the ability to predict a coming storm, however, nor does it even mean only the ability to see aspects of the land or the sky that "civilized" people cannot. Both of these are indeed aspects of the natural language about which we are speaking: every particular landscape and every particular changing sky reveals a kind of ambience or atmosphere. But the word *language* as used here implies preeminently the spiritual and psychic meanings in nature.

It is very difficult to translate from one human language to another; meaning is invariably lost, and it is lost irrevocably if the translator does not possess the spirit or heart of the original. This is one of many problems anthropologists have had in interpreting the religious traditions of the tribal peoples: a symbolic word or phrase in an Algonquian language may well convey worlds of meanings, but when translated into English the concepts appear flat and lifeless. For translation from one language to another to be truly effective, the spirit of the original must be maintained by the translator. If that spirit is there, then although the translation might be debatable on a literal level, the original implications can be preserved. So too, if the interpreter were truly religious in his or her own spiritual tradition, it would theoretically be possible to understand another tradition in a genuine way. But without a religious spirit, how could someone "translate" a tradition the heart of which he or she does not understand at all?

Precisely the same is true when speaking of the natural language of earth and sky. If we have no sense of the spiritual powers perpetually revealing themselves in nature, we simply cannot recognize the truths written in the world around us. The language of earth and sky—the spiritual truths inherent in nature—then has no existence for us. This is what is meant by the Iron Age as a description of our present era: we are hardened, dead to our world. We do not see what is quite literally before our very eyes. The Sun, the Wind, the Eight directions, the Waters, these have no spiritual meaning. They, like us, are merely objects.

Of course, so far we have been speaking of this language in abstract terms; and although it is necessary to do so, it is also important to remember that this language exists in a world of specifics: specific rivers, bends, rapids, specific trees, hills, caves, rock outcroppings, specific birds, animals, ears of corn. Indeed, someone has written that in the mid nineteenth century—during the last few years that the Pawnee could live freely on the Plains and during the last years of traditional ways—it was still understood that if half an ear of corn were thrown away, the corn would talk. It would speak of the wastefulness of the person who discarded it unthinkingly, and it may very well be that as a result of this wastefulness, corn would become scarce.[91] There is a direct relationship between waste and want; this is as true today as then. It is what the Buddhists call the irrefragable law of karma, of cause and effect.

There is a fundamental difference, however, between the abstract term *karma*, and the ear of corn speaking of the wasteful person who tossed it there: specificity. This specificity is revealed in the direct communication between the corn spirit and the human: there is an immediate psychic or subtle communication between people and the nonhuman beings who populate their world in the Amerindian universe. This is far from saying that such communication is absent in the Buddhist world. The point, rather, is that the Buddhist traditions and the Amerindian share the same fundamental understanding, but in Buddhism this understanding is part of an extraordinarily comprehensive doctrine; in the Amerindian tradition it remains a matter of psychic communication between beings.

The language of earth and sky—the language of the natural world—is one of reciprocation, of balance. But this language of reciprocity is foreign to modern people, who cannot understand and are repelled by Native traditions like the cutting of flesh from one's shoulders, or the piercing of the chest or back, as part of a spiritual practice. We no longer recognize that to receive, one must give of oneself. We only wish to receive; we are closed to our world and to the spirits everywhere within it. But this law of reciprocity governs the whole of nature, for it governs us and the spirits all around us.

Modern people look at virgin nature "aesthetically." "How beautiful a view!" Nixon exclaims, his motorcade stopped along a high road. "Someone should build a motel here." The natural world is something to be consumed for moderns; we wish to consume even the view, by rendering it frozen in photographs or other means of reproduction. But there is no "aestheticism" in a traditional people's view of the natural world. This is not to say that traditional peoples do not know beauty but rather that they know true beauty, beauty in context, and as spiritual manifestation.

The language of the earth is expressed in signs and symbols everywhere. The whole of nature is glyphs to be read, for within the rocks and trees and waters and sky are the spiritual powers that they body forth. In Buddhism, some spirits of nature are called *yaksas* and people undertake to pacify or bargain with them; one pays homage to trees in which powerful *yaksas* live by placing around them ritual platforms, flags, and offerings.[92] Not every place in nature is equally powerful—just as every little sapling is not necessarily the home of a powerful *yaksa*—but although there are certain places that possess a power such that one cannot avoid it, there are no insignificant places on this earth, for everywhere is *potentially* of spiritual significance.

Everywhere on earth there is a spiritual symbolic language. The sun reminds us of our spiritual Sun; the winds bespeak the breath of the Spirit; the waters remind us of the Waters above and the Waters below; the earth and the landscape about us remind us of the celestial paradise from which we are in a sense exiled. Forests, deserts, shores, mountains, all speak to us not just of their own physical existence but of the spiritual Origin of us all. Our natural world is translucent to the visionary, and the power of the visionary experience reverberates throughout the lifetime, being commemorated and reenacted in ceremonies.

The task we are set by all religious traditions, and in particular by our own, is to recognize what is truly at the heart of our spiritual practice, to truly see where and who we are. An autochthonous spiritual tradition like that of the Native Americans or the Australian Aborigines can reveal to us aspects of our own spiritual practices that have been ignored, can point us toward understanding our own place in this world with clarity and wisdom. This is not syncretism, exactly; it is rather a kind of spiritual gift that is given us near the end of an age. When all the world's religious traditions are eroding or being destroyed, it is still possible through divine grace to reconstruct what it means to be human.

At first, it might not seem possible for modern people, even if they are Christian, to relearn from nature the universal language of earth and sky. Alienated from the world around us and from our fellow beings, we moderns seem hell-bent on plundering this world and on utterly ignoring the spiritual traditions that have informed human existence since the beginning. But that which is universal can never be closed to us; it is only we who close ourselves off. In a sense we have chosen to live in this present world, for good or for ill. We are responsible for who and where we are, and the keys to understanding these things are always before us.

2
CElESTIAl AGRiCUlTURE,
CElESTIAl JOURNEy

Amerindian cultures have appeared in two primary forms: hunting, or nomadic, and sedentary, or agricultural. But these well-known fundamental differences in social structure represent adaptations to particular landscapes and conditions and not, as some have alleged, religious traditions completely foreign to one another. Native American religious traditions reflect a primordial unity that can be seen also among traditions far more geographically and temporally dispersed than the Amerindian, who after all share a common heritage. An examination of the Amerindian hunting and the agricultural traditions, then, may be expected to reveal not only tribes in whose lives both these traditions appear but also the metaphysical and cosmological understanding that links them.

At first it might appear that northern tribal cultures tended to embrace nomadic, hunting traditions, while southern cultures tended to be sedentary and agricultural. In some respects, of course, this is true: one certainly finds that South American and Central American traditions were based in vast urban ceremonial complexes, just as in the northern wilderness one finds much sparer, individualistic hunting traditions without the rich, almost overwhelming ritual symbolism of the south. But at the same time, one finds that in southern traditions, like the Aztec and the Mayan, hunting is highly significant, and so too in the Plains and eastern Woodlands of the Americas one finds hunting and agricultural traditions interwoven. It is perhaps useful to make categorical distinctions, but those categories rarely hold in reality.

Thus, rather than trying to categorize the various Amerindian traditions into such groups as nomadic and agrarian, it would no doubt be more useful to try to understand the metaphysical and cosmological significances inherent in nomadism and agrarianism as practiced. Modern people tend to approach Amerindian traditions from their own limited, materialistic perspective, and the South American and Central American traditional cultures especially have often been interpreted as though economic motives governed them in the same way they govern moderns. But from the traditional point of view, the way of life practiced in a particular tradition takes its significance not from its social, or even less from its economic justification, but from its metaphysical validation and from its cosmological meaning.

Nomadism and agrarianism represent the two lineages of humankind that stretch back into the furthest antiquity.[93] Even though many people today believe that first came hunters and then came farmers, in fact these two approaches to the natural world have an archetypal significance and are complementary. The nomadic hunting culture's mysteries are almost always affiliated with the sun, and the mysteries of the sedentary agricultural society are almost always affiliated with the moon. The mysteries of hunting are affiliated with the masculine; the mysteries of the earth are affiliated with the feminine.

What is more, hunting and agrarian rituals each contain elements of the other. The Plains Indian Sun Dance, for instance, requires four virginal girls for its inception. Conversely, the highest agricultural mysteries—though affiliated with the archetypal feminine and the earth—are in Native American traditions performed by the holy men. Among the Pawnee, the two kinds of mysteries—the hunting and the agricultural—corresponded in deep ways. The sacred Corn was considered "Mother of the People," but her mysteries were inaugurated by the finest buffalo hunter of the tribe, who had had a vision; and her mysteries, and the hunting mysteries, were parallel.

Both agrarian and hunting visionaries followed very nearly the same course: the hunting visionary was wrapped in a buffalo robe, and his virtuous conduct directly affected hunting success, just as the agricultural visionary was wrapped in a sacred robe, and his life was homologous with agricultural success for the duration of the season.[94] Here we see the two mysteries most clearly: the human world is indivisible with the spirit world through which the animals on the one hand, and the plants on the other, flourish or wane. The visionaries represent a direct link between the human and natural world and the spiritual realm.

To speak of two worlds here is of course a falsification; it is an intellectual construct we use to try to discuss what is happening in the mysteries of the Amerindian traditions during the annual rituals that reinforce, intensify, or support the rhythms of nature. It is perhaps more accurate to say that in the mysteries, the spirits inherent in the natural world are supported by us and in turn support us. That is, the human beings who live among the spirits in nature live purely, fulfill their vocation to be fully human, to realize their spiritual Origin; and because they do this, the spirits in turn agree to support humans. If we fulfill our hierophanic place in nature, nature in turn supports us physically.

When we abrogate this divine covenant and ignore our spiritual purpose, then there comes a plague upon the land, and humanity lives in spiritual and physical barrens, from which condition Jeremiah, like all prophets, calls us. Chief John Snow of the Stoney tribe wrote:

> We believe that the Creator made everything beautiful in his time. We believe that we must be good stewards of the Creator and not destroy nor mar His works of creation. We look upon stewardship not only in terms of money and the profit of a hundredfold, but in those of respect for the beauty of the land and of life in harmony with the succession of the seasons, so that the voices of all living things can be heard and continue to live and dwell among us. If an area is destroyed, marred, or polluted, my people say, the spirits will leave the area. . . . This is one of the greatest concerns of Indian people.[95]

Expressed in Christian terms, this is still fundamentally an Amerindian statement of values. When we do not fulfill our sacred purpose as divine vice-regents, when we do not take our axial position between above and below, but destroy through ignorance, then the spirits leave. Instead of a primordial, green, and beautiful land, one sees a dead landscape, unanimated in the purest sense of that word; there is a sense of desolation.

But how is it to live in a land the spirits inhabit? The answer is found in the terms *theagriculture* and *spiritual nomadism.* As an example of the agriculture: in lower Michigan, the first white settlers discovered that the Native Americans cultivated great circular "garden beds" of large and often ornate construction, great gardens in the form of wheels and spirals and other geometric forms, sometimes covering more than a square mile. Of course, once the tribes had been dispossessed, the farmers immediately ploughed these geometric gardens under and turned them into simple European fields. Today, in fact, not a single "garden wheel" remains; we possess only drawings or engravings of what they were.

To be sure, these geometric gardens served a certain practical purpose, in that cultivation was undertaken in patterns; crops were grown close together, so that there were not the great insect or disease problems that modern industrial monoculture farming entails; and then too, crops could be rotated according to a clear pattern. But more than these practical reasons inspired the great geometric gardens of the upper Midwest. To achieve the ends suggested here, one does not need beauty or intricate geometrical forms.

Above all, the geometric gardens of Native America, like the famous Persian gardens of the Middle East, reflected subtle and spiritual reality. Some have argued that the images of celestial paradises in Islam correspond to spiritualizations of earthly beauty—just as whites have spoken derisively of the Amerindian "happy hunting ground"—yet it is not true that earthly reality provides a model for paradise but rather that in a traditional culture, physical reality is made as much as possible to reflect its spiritual Origin and significance. Earth is made to reflect paradise, not paradise to reflect the earth.

The Persian gardens were patterned after and evoked the celestial gardens of paradise; by contemplating them, one was in fact contemplating and existing in the celestial gardens; they were a support for spiritual practice. In this regard, Shaikh Sadruddin Muhammad Shirazi wrote that

> of all the realities that man sees and contemplates in the world beyond, those which delight, like houris, castles, gardens, green vegetation, and streams of running water . . . none of these is extrinsic to him, to the very essence of his soul, none is distinct or separated from his own act of existing. . . . [For] we are concerned here with another realm of

existence, between which and the material world there is no relation as to *situs* or as to dimension.[96]

In the garden without is manifested an earthly reflection of the timeless and dimensionless spiritual or celestial garden.

The same is true of the Amerindian gardens: in their geometrical forms were the physical manifestations of spiritual reality. Since in Native American traditions generally, ritual practice was revealed in visions, one can hardly doubt that these geometric forms were originally revealed in visionary glimpses of the celestial powers that govern the growing corn and other plants. Likewise, the petroglyphs in sacred rocks manifested what was revealed in vision to the nomad: the spiritual archetypes governing the animals. In a sense, the geometric gardens were terraglyphs that embodied spiritual reality; they represented the earth redeemed into paradisal reality. To tend them was to tend the spirits and deities themselves; in the gardens, as in the petroglyphs and other sacred sites, the veil between celestial and earthly reality is more translucent.

Iroquois tradition in this vein is illuminating, for according to it—as according to Persian spiritual tradition—all terrestrial phenomena reflect eternal *ongwe,* "elder brothers," or archetypes. There are animal archetypes like Deer, Fawn, Bear, Beaver; theagrarian archetypes like Corn, Bean, Squash, and Sunflower; celestial archetypes like Aurora Borealis, Star Spirits, and many more. These archetypes live in a celestial longhouse (of which the ritual longhouse is a physical reflection); to farm is therefore not merely "working the land" but is theagrarian or ritual practice.[97]

This mythology has profound cosmological significance. According to Seneca tradition—as in all religious traditions—there is a prehistorical celestial reality, and there are celestial "events" that resulted in the creation of this physical world. The most significant of these "events" was the fall of one of the archetypal celestial beings from the paradisal state near the Axis of being. Reminiscent of the Fall of Sophia depicted in Gnostic Christian and Mandaean cosmology, in Senecan cosmology it is said that there was a celestial kingdom near the Tree of the Worlds, and in it was a chief. This chief could make the kingdom, which was something like a cloud, move at will.[98] The chief took a young wife, named Sky Woman, or Mature Flowers; she became pregnant; and they both grew curious about what was beneath the great World Tree. The chief lifted the Tree up, Mature Flowers sat near the hole—and the chief pushed her in. She "fell to earth"; she is the "ancestor" of earthly beings. From her came the Twins, Good and Evil; through her corporeal earth became as we know it today, with grasses, plants, trees, animals, people. But to this day, we can see through this physical world—as in a reflection of the Sky in a pool of water—the archetypal Reality from which it fell.

Just as in a traditional culture to farm is not merely a physical but a subtle and spiritual practice, so also to hunt and to make journeys is not merely physical in significance. All human activities in a sacred tradition remind us of this spiritual realm that is our Origin. Some writers have disparaged nomadic traditions as primitive or marauding; others have disparaged agrarian cultures as sedentary and as the origin of that sprawling urban nightmare, the modern city. And indeed, when decadent—when severed from their spiritual or archetypal significance—both nomadism and agrarianism may be merely "marauding" or "sedentary." Yet to the extent that either kind of tradition retains its spirituality and to the extent that its physical environs remain pristine, such a tradition remains not just a way of life but a spiritual path connecting earth and heaven.

If the agriculture reveals how the dynamic informs the unchanging—or stable—agrarian world, the spiritual journeys of nomads reveal how stability—or the unchanging—appears in their dynamic travels. While the agrarians stay in a single place, in that place the dynamic powers of nature inform and empower their gardens, whose growth follows cycles of time. Likewise, while nomads move through space, there are throughout that space the signs of the eternal or timeless. Hence, the more agrarian culture tends to develop a richer "outward" or symbolic tradition, while the more nomadic culture tends to develop a richer "inward" or oral tradition. The agrarians tend toward making their stable world conform to spiritual reality while the nomads tend toward maintaining the stable oral or inward traditions that allow them to recognize the signs of the timeless in the landscape through which they move.

For the nomads, the earth is itself the manifestation of the sacred Word; to move through the land is to move through a world charged with spiritual and psychic truth. This is why to restrict the nomads, to keep them locked up within square houses, in a square lot, along a street, is to destroy not just their freedom of movement but their spiritual tradition. For them, the rock escarpments, the sacred springs, the mountains, the groves, these are not just natural phenomena but the actual manifestations in the physical world of spiritual and psychic power. This is why every nomadic tradition has such an extensive orally transmitted mythology; the recital of the mythological liturgy does not transform the landscape for the nomads but rather reveals to them the sacred truth embodied in that land or place. Physical journeys are therefore spiritual and psychic journeys as well.[99]

Hence, when we consider the Amerindian traditions in their totality, we must recognize the operative principle that informs them all; for through these religious traditions, the physical world reveals the spiritual archetypes that are not just its vital power but are "translucent" and reveal the spiritual Origin of all things. This is as true of theagriculture as it is of nomadic journeys. Native American spiritual traditions are essential if modern Americans are ever to make peace with this continent to which we have come but with which we still have so little rapport.

For modern civilization, agriculture is merely a method of producing food; traveling is merely a matter of "going somewhere" or of "tourism." If, however, we wish to see the world in any more profound way—and if for that matter we wish to avoid complete destruction—we must come to recognize that we are not merely physical beings in a physical world. We must recognize that sacred mountains have a significance and influence far beyond their monetary worth as places to mine or lumber or dump; that our roads, if they must be built, must not go through a sacred place; that our sacred springs must not be destroyed; that sacred rivers must not be dammed, flooding sacred caves and rock escarpments. The destruction of such places is sign and seal of our spiritual impoverishment.

We may like to think that we can escape this world and travel through outer space to another that we have not yet destroyed. But it would be infinitely better instead to understand the significance of Christ's admonition: "Lay not up for yourselves treasures upon earth, where moth and rust doth corrupt, and where thieves break through and steal: But lay up for yourselves treasures in heaven"[100]—and consider deeply how this admonition corresponds to the Native American traditions of theagriculture and spiritual nomadism.

3
Spiritual Landscape

It is more and more uncommon for modern people to be *from* a particular landscape. Unrooted, we move from place to place as though the land in which we live is virtually disposable and certainly interchangeable. This diaspora reveals the fundamental instability and spiritual blindness of modern civilization generally, and of Americans in particular. Modern Americans, with our mercantilist mentality, believe that one can buy and sell everything, that the physical land is all. But for the original peoples, existence in this world is a spiritual pilgrimage, and the landscape itself is spiritual.

It is hardly necessary to discuss the spiritual blindness inherent in modern civilization's relentless destruction of the natural world. No one who possessed the slightest awareness of nature's transcendent significance could drive a bulldozer at a sacred site, gouge away at a sacred rock, or cut down all the trees in a wood to put up cheap square houses all in rows. As a Lakota Sioux holy man put it: white is the color of the north, of the cruel north wind. Merciless, the white race destroys. There is only one cure for this rapaciousness: re-cognition of the sacredness of landscape.

To rediscover the spiritual landscape that surrounds us, we must first realize our place in that landscape as spiritual pilgrims. A pilgrim is one who goes on a journey to holy land, to sacred land, and from the time of the first English settlers, America was seen by whites as a New Jerusalem, as a new holy land, as a potential Paradise, to which the whites were pilgrims. Unfortunately, this sense of pilgrimage—of making a journey through a holy land—quickly was converted into a desire to conquer, to *own*. But by definition, no one can own a place of pilgrimage. Rather, such a place gives freely to all.

In the spirituality of the original peoples, one is irrefutably *from* a particular spiritual landscape, and to be separated from that place is to be separated from one's spiritual origin. The Pottawatomi were driven from the Great Lakes to Kansas several generations ago, but the elders still speak of their homeland by the Great Lakes. So too, if you speak of home to a dislocated Pueblo, she will speak of the open horizon she has lost; if you speak to a dislocated Macaw, he will speak of the great trees of home. This homesickness is a spiritual homesickness; dislocation is in many ways the most destructive of the means used to destroy the spirituality of the Amerindian peoples.

In the traditional view, we are from a particular spiritual landscape; and yet we are a pilgrims within it. We do not own the land; the spirit of the land possesses us. We are born of a particular clan, or spiritual ancestral line, and of a particular spiritual landscape. Modern people might believe that genetics or conditioning are all that produces a given child or adult; but in reality, we are each born of a special spiritual ambience. This is why a Pottawatomi grandmother might say "Wayahgeisuk is come" when a child is born; she knows through dream, vision, or other means the essential pattern or nature of the one who has come, that of which the child was born and which the child reflects. She even knows the child's name.

To be born of a particular spiritual landscape—to be a pilgrim within it— means that one travels through life as through the landscape. One's purpose on earth is not to own or control the natural world but to deepen one's character and to realize spiritual truth in one's own life. This recognition is why the original peoples regarded their bodies with what appears to us as ascetic callousness. The spiritual import of one's life was considered far more important than one's mere body; if fasting or self-lacerating or driving the pegs of the Sun Dance through the chest muscles, back muscles, or leg muscles was necessary to the spiritual journey, then so be it.

Central to that journey is often a high place. Those remains of sacred sites still left to us in the Great Plains of America are almost invariably on the highest ground in the surrounding countryside, and from them one can see the whole horizon, the ringed land laid out in every direction. Often too, it is said by local people in such a place that their area is kept safe by that high ground, and even though such comments are made with an under-current of scoffing, still they are made, and continue to be made, for there are certain truths or awarenesses embedded in the very psyche, despite our modern conditioning. People intuitively know that a sacred high place emanates a protective influence over the land around it.

Such an influence corresponds to the tradition among virtually all the Plains Indians of retreating to a high place and "lamenting" or calling upon the Divine power to take pity on one, to offer a vision. The combined spiritual efforts of thousands of vision seekers to call upon the Divine in such a place reinforces or intensifies its spiritual irradiation or conductivity. This is why in many local traditions these high places are seen as protecting the nearby land from tornadoes or high winds or other kinds of destructive weather.

There are other kinds of spiritual landscapes: woodland, island, and waterfront places that are sacred too. Throughout New England and the Midwest, for example, and especially in New York State, early white settlers found the remains of what they often called "Indian forts"—raised earth embankments, often circular, often facing a bend in a river below. These were not forts—they had nothing to do with battles, for the embankments were often far too low for that, and in any case Amerindian warfare did not proceed in European fashion, as if one tribe were storming another's castle. These embankments instead represent an intensification of the energy in a particular landscape, a place of spiritual practice.

These kinds of embankments appeared on knolls and near flowing water because in such a place the autochthonous energy—what the Chinese call *ch'i*, and the Iroquois *orenda*—could accumulate. In Michigan, for example, there is a hill overlooking a bend in the Grand River on which was the only embankment in that county. Directly to the east-northeast is a group of burial mounds; flowing from northeast to southwest is the river. That sandy knoll was the site of a circular embankment used by the nearby villages as a place of spiritual contact with the divine powers; it was conducive to such contact because the spiritual energy of the place was intensified by that site. Similar sites are found throughout eastern and midwestern America.

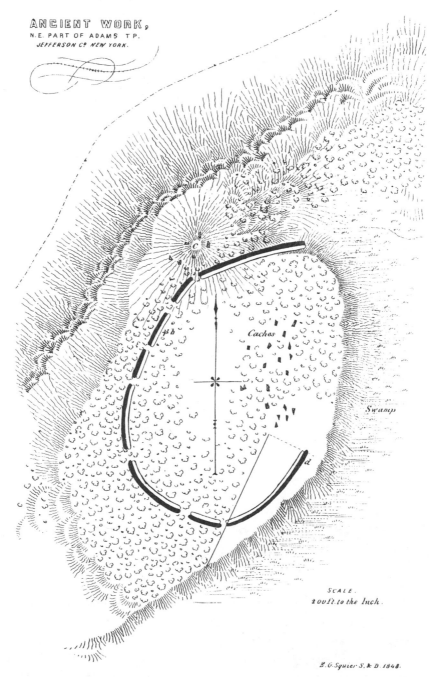

ANCIENT WORK,
N.E. PART OF ADAMS TP.
JEFFERSON Cº NEW YORK.

Caches

Swamp

SCALE.
200 ft. to the Inch.

E. G. Squier S. & D. 1848.

An ancient earthwork of New York State, situated on a high point in Jefferson County. The earthwork is open to the east. From Squier, Antiquities of the State of New York, *1851.*

ANCIENT WORK,
CLARENCE TP. ERIE COUNTY N.Y.
1½ Mile S.W. of Clarence Hollow.

E.G.S.1848
N.º 2

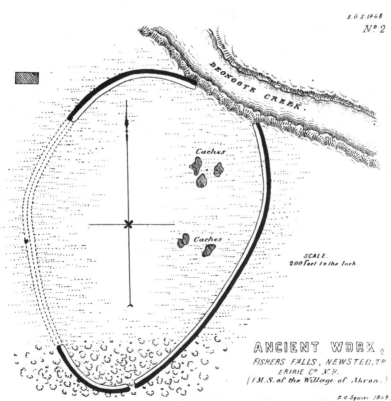

DEONOOTE CREEK.

Caches

Caches

SCALE.
200 feet to the Inch

ANCIENT WORK,
FISHERS FALLS, NEWSTED, TP.
ERIRIE C.º N.Y.
(1 M.S. of the Village of Akron.)

E.G. Squier 1848.

More geognostically situated earthworks, again on higher ground, opening out to flowing waters. Such sites have deep correspondences to the Chinese science of feng shui, or sacred landscape. From Squier, Antiquities, 1851.

Certain rocks or caves also have a special significance. Rocks or stones generally are recognized by original peoples all over the world as possessing a metaphysical significance, in that they are the crystallization of the Primal Substance of the cosmos, and this is especially true of certain rocks. In England one finds many standing stones put in celestial patterns, which body forth an awareness of the bond between sky and earth, between celestial and terrestial. In the Americas this same awareness is reflected not (for the most part) in artificially raised stones but in great rocks that have stood since time immemorial.

Pawnee Rock in Kansas exemplifies one such sacred lithic, although there are many affiliated sacred sites. Still standing, Pawnee Rock was one of several Plains sites in Pawnee legend to which the spirits of the animals, or Nahu'rac, went for conclave, in a hole in the rock.[101] The rock was called Pa-hur', or "Hill That Points the Way." There were traditionally four other such sites within Pawnee territory, all of them within the earth rather than in a sacred stone; all of the other sites were along rivers. One was Pa-huk', or "Hill Island," on the south side of the Platte River in Nebraska; another was Lalawakohtito, or "Dark Island," beneath an island on the Platte River near Central City; the third was Ahkawitakol, or "White Bank," on the Loup Fork opposite the mouth of the Cedar River; and the fourth was Pa'howa, or Kitzawitzuk, meaning "Water on the Bank," a mound in which was a hole into the watery underworld, found on the Solomon River. Like Pawnee Rock, here the animal spirits met for conclave, and here offerings could be made.

Hence, wherever the Pawnee traveled during their nomadic hunting lives, so long as they remained within the landscape marked by these sites they were living in a visionary or spiritual geography. By making offerings at these sacred places and by remaining in continuous, cyclic contact with them, they were also able to remain in contact with the spiritual forces that manifested as the animals upon which they depended for food, clothing, and much else. Looking at these sites today—many of them decimated or ruined by the whites—means little to us, for they appear only as they are, as ruined, small places in a vast land. But for the tribal people, these sites loom much larger in the mind, as centers in a rich spiritual geography, as places where spiritual powers congregate.

For all the original peoples, the world spread out around us is not only marked by places of spiritual congregation but is stretched out upon the rood

of space, which together with the above and below of the vertical Axis forms
the six directions. Each of the four cardinal directions is in fact a spiritual
power, with all its affiliated colors, associations, and cosmological implications. The cross in Amerindian traditions, as in Muslim, Hindu, and other
traditions, possesses not a historical but a cosmological significance, and
it embodies our situation on this earth as spiritual pilgrims in a sacred
geography.[102]

Different tribes possess slightly different rescensions of the same directional symbolism, corresponding no doubt to the geographical differences
in the landscapes they inhabit. Generally speaking, however, in the west
is blue or black, in the north is white, in the east is red, and in the south
is yellow.[103] In the vision of Black Elk, the two roads on which a person
can walk are the west-east axis, which is the black road of suffering and
materialism, and the south-north axis, which is the red road that leads to
serenity and transcendence.[104] In Black Elk's words, one who travels the
west-east road is "one who is distracted, who is ruled by his senses, and
who lives for himself rather than for his people."[105]

To follow the red road is to follow the straight and narrow path; it is to
move toward the Axis of the worlds, which is in the north. One faces south,
the direction of life, during life; but to transcend the whirl of suffering that
is existence, one follows the Milky Way home toward the Pole of Life in
the north. This is the red road; it is the vertical direction transposed onto
the horizontal place; to go north is to go Upward. This is why white is the
northern color; it is the color and the direction of purification, and to ascend
one must be purified. All of this symbolism corresponds to Hindu, Buddhist,
and Taoist directional symbolism in its fundamental meaning, if not in every
detail.[106]

This directional symbolism is at the heart of Amerindian traditions, and
whether or not it is also transposed into the semicardinal directions, the
essential meaning remains the same. Wherever one walks on earth, one is
walking in a cosmos circumscribed not only by the rim of the world but
by the Powers that exist in each of its corners. If alchemists wish to consider
the meaning of the "squaring of the circle," they would do well to consider
the aboriginal understanding of the horizon's circle and the directional
square, for here, where we walk, is everywhere the squaring of the circle.

Above us is the circle, representing the completeness of our spiritual
Origin, shown to us in the horizon's ring; where we stand is the human
realm, marked by the directional cross, or by the figure of a man with his

arms outstretched; and below us is the square or the cube of earth, or Primal Substance. Here then is the Amerindian representation of our place in the cosmos: here we have the three worlds, called in Hindu tradition *svah*, *bhuvah*, and *bhuh*, or Sky, Atmosphere, and Earth—Celestial, Subtle, and Physical reality. Below is the Rock, the Primal Substance, and above is the Celestial reality of the sky, to show us the spiritual Essences, or patterns, that our cosmos reflects.

This symbolic representation of the cosmos was manifested very precisely in the villages of the Creeks in southeastern North America, as writer Ephraim Squier depicted in 1851. In the heart of every village was a circular lodge, or rotunda, in which the holiest ceremonies were practiced. This represents the celestial realm; the profane could not enter. In terms of the human body, this represents the head, and the prohibition of the unclean corresponds to the widespread prohibition among many tribes against touching or scratching one's head during spiritual practices.[107] One does not touch the head any more than one profanes the *sanctum sanctorum*; to do so means self-consciousness or egotism, and the purpose of spiritual practice and of the celestial lodge is self-transcendence.

Before the circular lodge is a semicardinally arranged series of central lodges that form a square. Since this square of lodges is designed with one corner pointing toward the rotunda and one pointing down to the main village square below it, with spaces between, one can see all the way from the village square, between the lodges, to the rotunda, or ceremonial lodge, just as one can "see through" the subtle realm that this intermediate set of lodges represents. The four corners of the square formed by the lodges point toward the four directions, and the four sides of the lodges point to the semicardinal directions, forming an octagon.

At the opposite end of the village from the circular lodge or rotunda was the great village square, in which one would find a large ceremonial pole and two smaller poles, arranged in triangular form. The large pole, called a *chung-kye* pole, had been raised on a mound, and with the two other poles formed the area for the sacred game of *chung-kye*, played with rods and a ball. *Chung-kye*, like *tapa wanka yap*, the Lakota ball game about which Black Elk talks at the end of *The Sacred Pipe*, "was not really a game, but one of our most important sacred rites." According to Black Elk,

> The game . . . represents the course of a man's life, which should be spent
> in trying to get the ball, for the ball represents *Wakan-Tanka*, or the

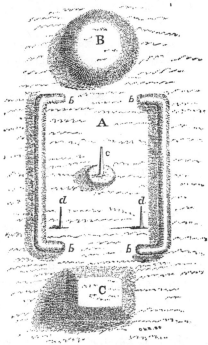

The center of a Creek village in the southeastern United States. B is the rotunda mound, signifying the circle of sky; in the center is the chunk-yard, or open area, signifying atmosphere, and below is the square, signifying earth; "chunk poles" are also shown. From Squier, Antiquities, 1851.

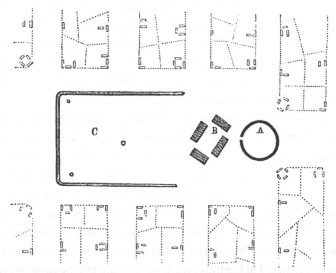

Another view of a Creek village, showing the houses surrounding the center yard. This is a variation on the same symbolism as above: we see the symbolism of sky, atmosphere, and earth. The village represents a mesocosm, a reflection of the cosmos as a whole. From Squier, Antiquities, 1851.

universe, as I shall explain later. In the game today it is very difficult to get the ball, for the odds—which represent ignorance—are against you, and it is only one or two of the teams who are able to get the ball and score with it. But in the original rite everyone was able to have the ball, and if you think about what the ball represents, you will see that there is much truth in it.[108]

One played *chung-kye* on the large village square, which in cosmological terms represents earth, the physical realm; the ball with which the game was played represents eternity, or the transcendent. The form of the three poles recapitulates the emanation of the cosmos from the Axis "outward" into duality.

All of this corresponds in striking ways to Buddhist and Hindu traditional symbolism. In a Buddhist *stupa,* or religious monument, one finds precisely the same symbolism: above is the dome, or circle; below that is the octagonal base on which it sits; and below that is the cube, representing earth.[109] Likewise, as René Guénon points out, this same symbolism recurs both in Christian and in Hindu traditions: the octagon, in Hinduism connected with Vayu, the winds, is intermediate between the celestial and terrestrial realms.[110]

Hence, to play the game was not merely an entertainment, something merely to fill time; rather, the game, like every other aspect of traditional life, was a religious rite, filled with spiritual meaning. Indeed, to play the game corresponds to the pilgrimage of one's life; the game was a distilled or condensed form of life itself, just as the triform village center of the Creeks reflects the threefold nature of the cosmos.

The key to the spiritual journey across the landscape in which we find ourselves is understanding that the meaning of any landscape—for all the differences in terrain and particularity—is its reflection of fundamental, eternal truth. This is why one finds such striking, astonishing correspondences independent of circumstances; that which is revealed within the context of particular traditions always corresponds to eternal verities. The Lakota Sioux game of which Black Elk speaks was the seventh and last revealed rite of the White Buffalo Woman and came in a vision to a man who then revealed it to the tribe; yet its symbolism corresponds to ball games played over all the Americas. Truth is independent of circumstances but is revealed according to particular situations or ambiences.

This universality revealed in particularities is the heart of our spiritual journey's meaning, of the spiritual landscape that surrounds us. A tree is a tree, but it also is the Axis of the worlds; a mountain is a mountain, but it also is the Mountain at the center of all worlds; a ridge is only a ridge, but it also is the serpentine power of the earth spirit made physical before us, and that bluff is indeed its head. These are not merely acts of imagination, mere fantasy. Rather, the landscape through which we make our pilgrimage and the spiritual reality it symbolizes are one and the same.

4

MOUNTAINS AND FIRE,
WINDS AND WATERS

Mountains and winds, earth, waters, and fire all have spiritual significances in the world religious traditions: every land has its sacred mountains, its holy rivers, its sanctified places. Jesus Christ went upon the mount to give his sermon; Buddhists and Hindus alike make pilgrimages to sacred mountains in the Himalayas; the Ganges is a sacred river; for the Greeks the Gods dwelled on Mount Olympus; the Irish have their Tara; and in the Americas too are sacred mountains, holy rivers, and sacred places.[111]

To realize the celestial meaning common to sacred mountains, sacred winds, sacred waters, sacred earth, and sacred fire, we might look to a symbol common to many tribes, that which among the Pawnee symbolized Tirawa, the Supreme Spirit. During certain rituals, the Pawnee would paint on the human head an arch up from the cheekbones and over the forehead. From the center of this arch descended a line down the bridge of the nose.[112] This symbolized the dome of heaven, and the line down the center signified the descent of the Spirit, of which rain is symbolic. It is said among the Pawnee that this line down the center extends to the heart of the human being, and it means that the person is connected directly to the Great Spirit above.

This symbol is not only common to many tribes, but indeed it is universal, for analogous symbols are found in different forms in all the world religions. The implications of the symbol may in fact be best explained by reference to Hindu and Buddhist traditions, and in particular to their yogic and cosmological meanings, for exactly the same symbolism of the arch and the descending line are found in the Hindu and Buddhist symbol called the *kalamakara,* or serpent balustrade, rising up over the entrance to many Asian temples. The serpents rise alongside the stairs and up over the arch of the doorway, where they meet in a single face, the "Face of Time," or the "Face of glory," from which falls the *amrita,* or Divine Nectar.[113]

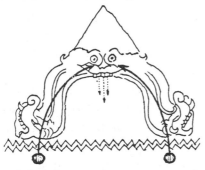

A kalamakara, *a figure over temple entranceways in Java, showing the currents from the waters below rising upward to the head, and the* amrita, *or Divine Nectar falling from above. This same pattern is recapitulated in the rain cycle of nature and in certain yogic practices.*

The Pawnee symbol for Tirawa, or the Supreme Spirit. The arch is the dome of the sky; it is painted on the forehead in a blessing ceremony, and the line runs down the bridge of the nose to the heart. From the Twenty-second Annual Report of the Bureau of American Ethnology.

This path of the serpentine powers up to the temple entrance corresponds to the rising of the spiritual energy in the yogin, or spiritual practitioner, and to the drops of spiritual nectar, or *amrita,* coming from above. There is a direct correlation between the macrocosm and the microcosm visible in the temple itself; the temple reveals how spiritual energy rises upward to the peak of the arch, and how it descends from heaven. Precisely the same symbolism is seen in the mysterious way water ascends into the heavens and falls as rain—metaphysical symbolism is always precisely congruent with natural symbolism. This symbolism also corresponds to the individual, as in the Pawnee face painting. By prayer and purification, the individual realizes in himself or herself the same spiritual power that is revealed externally in the forces of nature and in religious symbolism. This power is revealed in the heart, hence the line from the heart to heaven.

This same symbol also may be said to represent the sacred mountain and the path of ascent and descent. In the center is the axis and also the path to the summit, which is simultaneously the "sun door" or "cosmic exit" through the celestial arch. The central line in the symbol represents at once the ascent of the individual upward, toward the Transcendent beyond the celestial dome, and the descent of spiritual power through the celestial ministers, to people and to earth. This is why Tirawa is said to be inaccessible directly by a human being and has intermediate ministers, much in the way that in Christian theology one has the Godhead, then God, then the hierarchies of Angels in descending order to human life upon earth.[114]

The symbol discussed here represents, as does the Asian symbol of the *kalamakara*, the connections between the sacred mountain and the sacred waters. For the waters rise up as mist and form clouds, from which falls the sacred rain. And although Tirawa is "beyond the clouds," Tirawa's power manifests in the clouds and rain as well, for without these things human beings and earthly creatures could not live. Rain symbolizes a "message from heaven to earth," and in Christian terms represents "Revelation, and also Grace." Thus, as Black Elk said, "whenever the truth of vision comes on the world, it is like a rain."[115] And the sacred rains come from over the mountains onto the great plains in the Americas.

Finally, this symbol recalls the symbolism of fire, for the plume of smoke rises from the fire upward into the heavens. The sacred fire is therefore called the sacred messenger; the fire is a witness and knows what is said around it. When one makes an offering to the sacred fire, it carries the sacrifice and the message it entails upward to the spirit world, to the celestial realm represented by the dome. The fire corresponds to the heart in humans; both of them convey what is good or bad in humans and in our actions. The sacred fire is the manifestation on earth of celestial light, just as the heart is the manifestation of the celestial ray extending downward from heaven through the human being.

In this single glyph, then—a dome from which extends a single ray downward—is condensed the spiritual meanings of the mountains and of the waters and of fire, all of which correspond to the human microcosm, to the symbolism of the head and the heart. In the Cheyenne Great Lodge, this symbol is painted near the buffalo skull at the lodge's altar, corresponding to the same symbol painted on the Pawnee face and to the spiritual landscape that surrounds and informs both of these. Spiritual landscape is not merely outside us; it informs nature, the ritual world, and the human microcosm all at once. If nature is the macrocosm, and humanity the microcosm, then ritual is the mesocosm, intermediate between people and nature, as between people and the spirits.

We have discussed in an earlier context how certain places manifest especial power. There are translucent places through which the spiritual landscape is particularly visible: petroglyph sites, for instance, or sacred mountains. Still others are domes or mounds in which waters rise, as in the case of Wakonda Spring in Kansas, the most sacred place in that area and revered by all tribes. (The spring is now at the bottom of Glen Elder Reservoir, because of a dam built some years ago.) These sites are particularly sacred because there the spirit realm is closest to the human world.

Of course, power is power, and from a human perspective its manifestations may be either beneficial or destructive. One may be blessed or blasted by the same power, a truth which is expressed mythologically in the Iroquois myth of the twin sons, called Good Mind and Evil Mind. In this myth, both beneficent and destructive power emanate from the same mother, and while one son goes around creating good things, the other son goes around laying waste, creating obstacles, and producing unnatural or poisonous creatures. Both this myth and a similar one in the Persian mythology of Ohrmazd and Ahriman suggest how sacred power can be perceived as beneficent and as destructive.[116]

Part of the cosmological truth that makes such myths so instructive is the law of complementarity in the cosmos. Everything balances. Hence, even though many tribal people fear the water spirits, nonetheless, in some tribal traditions it is said that from the water spirits come sacred rituals. Among the Algonquin of the Great Lakes, for instance, it is said that the horned water snakes drowned Little Wolf, brother of the cultural hero, and so in recompense to humanity, the horned water snakes gave the tribe the medicine lodge and rites to prolong life and to secure a good afterlife. While the water snakes appear malevolent in drowning Little Wolf, in the end they prove beneficial to humanity.[117] Likewise, the Shoshoni fear to even point a finger at the Grand Tetons, precisely because they are sacred mountains and body forth spiritual power.[118]

The essence of these examples is that all sacred landscape—earth, air, water, or rock—manifests spiritual power and so must be approached with reverence and caution. One gives an offering to the spirits of the lake; one makes an offering to the spirits in the mountains; one gives tribute to the spirits of the winds and to the guardians because they possess greater power than human beings, and because they can both bless or blast. Reverence and caution are complementary results of knowledge, and in both Amerindian and Taoist traditions it is said that one must be careful when venturing into mountains or other sacred places.

Humanity's place in this world is as Repairer, as the one who reverently acts as intermediary between heaven and earth. This truth has been repeated again and again by Native American leaders; the eloquence of Big White Owl of the Delaware Indians is characteristic:

> We who live in this period of ever-changing panorama cannot fully comprehend the mystery and sublimity of Kitche Manitou's great plan; we can only wait, patiently and quietly, for we know that Kish-lamo-k'wang [the Creator] works in strange and mysterious ways His wonders to perform.
>
> Today, as I look out over the vastness of this land, I can see upon the ruins and ashes of our once peaceful villages and ancient council-fires, that a nation of pale-faced people have built a new kind of civilization which seems to be emblazoned with four terrifying and all-consuming monsters: Greed, Prejudice, Hate, Fear. And I find, to my great sorrow, that this new civilization is dissolving into itself, ruthlessly and destructively, all the silent restful places of the land. It seems to have found some sort of romance in converting and diverting the powers of Nature into implements of devastation and destruction. This new way of life is mutilating and destroying and robbing the fertility of our precious soil! Must we of the Lenni Lenape forever sit back and watch this chaos with impassive eyes?
>
> Down through all the painful centuries we have been taught by our wise ones to regard ourselves as mediators and arbitrators. It was our duty to lead the fighting and wayward Indian nations into the ways of peace and brotherhood. We were the sentinels and scouts. We were the trailblazers and the peace-makers. We were the official keepers of the sacred fire of peace, which was handed to our Fire Builders from an altar beyond

the horizon of time. . . . Brothers and friends, let us, in this troubled period, once more hold high the torch of liberty and peace! . . . Let us save America! I have spoken.[119]

As civilization ruthlessly destroys all the silent restful places of the land, even mountains and waters seem unable to stand against modern depredations. But humanity's task remains the same: we are the keepers of the sacred fire of peace, handed down from an altar beyond the horizon of time.

To accomplish this task, humans act as intermediaries between the different realms. This is why, in many Indian traditions across America, it is said that visionaries are admitted into a conference of the spirits that takes place under the waters of a river or a lake, or beneath the earth, or in a sacred rock or mountain, or up in the skies. At first it would seem that these are such disparate places they must refer to completely different things, but in fact the fundamental principle of such meetings remains the same. Whether the spirit meeting place is beneath sacred waters, in a sacred mountain, or in the heavens—whether it is in the kingdom of the water, of the earth, or of the air—it is a meeting of the archetypal spirits and the human soul in a spiritual landscape.

Whether it be indicated to us through a symbol like that for Tirawa, or whether it be experienced directly, as has been the case for countless tribal people over the centuries, the visionary landscape is not somewhere to which we can escape but is the reality of the world in which we already live. As Black Elk put it, indicating with his hand Harney Peak, which he had seen in his most powerful vision, "Right over there is where I stood in my vision, but the hoop of the world about me was different, for what I saw was in the spirit."[120] In this seeing in the spirit is the meaning of the human place in this world and of the mountains and the waters of many colors.

5
THE COUNCIL FIRE

It has long been a tradition, among many tribes, that there be a sacred fire—
or at times a tree or a rock—that can act as a witness to what is said in
council at that place. The tree, the rock, or the fire "ground," or center, those
who meet there; the witness orients the participants, and it is to that witness
that they come. The center is an axis; it connects earth and heaven, people
and nature and spirits. And at that axial center, Judeo-Christian America and
the Native American religious traditions meet.

These traditions of course do not always coincide exoterically. Indeed,
there is a proselytizing element within evangelical Christianity that to the
present day cannot acknowledge the legitimacy of any religion other than
the Christian. Yet even on the level of religious teaching, Christianity is in
certain respects quite foreign to the Native American traditions. The doctrine
of vicarious atonement, for example—that Christ came to save all people
from their sins—is strange to a tradition in which everyone has direct
experiential contact with the Divine, in which virtually everyone is enjoined
to fast and seek visions for the tribe as a whole, and in which there is no
equivalent to the Christian concept of a Redeemer for all of humanity

(although tribal traditions are constantly being renewed). Then too, Christianity is a tradition of the Book. The Book of the Native American is nature herself, nature's spirits. In many ways, Christianity and Native American traditions make a study in contrasts.

Of course, many of the conflicts between Europeans and Indians had virtually nothing to do with Christianity in its true sense. Men like Pizarro and Cortez claimed to be Christians fighting battles of the Faith against the Native Americans, but despite the absolution of the conquerors by militant priests, the fact remains that they were really slaughtering Amerindians, as Cortez himself said, "for our honor, for riches, for revenge." One could count riches highest in this trinity. When Pizarro massacred thousands upon thousands of unarmed Incas in Peru, and his men looted the bodies; and when Cortez's men fell upon the Aztec nobles during a sacred dance in a temple, butchered them so that the pavement "ran with streams of blood, like water in a heavy shower," and then looted the bodies and the temples, one could find no motivation other than naked greed and evil. To Pizarro's massacre of thousands, his chaplain Valverde, a Dominican friar, commanded: "Set on at once; I absolve you."[121]

Modern history in the Americas is shameful not least because the unmitigated evils perpetrated against the native peoples often were committed under the guise of Christianity. Indeed, when one contemplates the whole history of "Christian" slaughter, thievery, dispossession, and atrocities committed against the original peoples—not to mention the erosion, outlawing, and obliteration of sacred religious traditions—the relentless perfidy of it all is fairly inconceivable. One could not recount all the evils perpetrated by "civilization" against the Native Americans from the first European contact to the present day. From the Puritans burning Indians to death inside barricaded churches, to the giving of blankets infected with smallpox to tribespeople, to the mutilation of corpses, to the slaughter of entire villages, to the abrogation of treaty after treaty, to the obliteration of the buffalo to eliminate the Prairie Indians, to the forced marches to "reservations," to forced sterilization, to the destruction of sacred lands by mining and other corporate interests, to the countless shameful acts of the Bureau of Indian Affairs—the recital of sins is veritably endless.

All of this destruction—though often undertaken in the guise of Christianity—had nothing to do with that religion as spiritual experience. It was not in truth Christianity but materialistic modern civilization that stood opposed to and destroyed the Native American traditions and peoples. It is not insignificant that the Christians who so industriously set about to proselytize by murder knew nothing of their own mystical tradition, nothing of the spiritual experiences attested to by Eckhart and Tauler, Suso and Böhme. The grim, exoteric, literalist faith embraced by so many Americans bears only a tangential and tenuous relationship to the rich spiritual life of Christian mysticism, which is far closer to Native American religious traditions than one might at first think.

Americans are not truly at home in this, their still-adopted land. They have not come to terms with their own history, with their own religious heritage, or with the original peoples and their spiritual understanding of life and land. Still we destroy the land; still we ignore our rich spiritual inheritance; still we seek material gain and ignore the kingdom at hand. The hour is late. But visionary revelation is not foreign to Christianity, as the Johannine Revelation shows; inner spiritual experience on the order of an Eckhart or a Tauler is not closed to us; the worlds of angels, spirits, elementals, and demons have not disappeared, we have only grown blind to them.

At an inner or experiential level, there cannot but be common ground between the religious traditions, just as there is a council fire or axis to which various tribes are oriented, and at which they can meet. The axis to which all traditions are oriented is divine revelation; and if in Christianity this revelation is mediated through Christ, in the Amerindian traditions it is mediated through nature. It is in nature that the original peoples find spiritual revelation; yet this is not absent from Christianity, as the example of St. Francis of Assisi demonstrates. And conversely, although Christianity tends to take institutional forms not found among the Native Americans, yet there are corresponding initiatory traditions and hierarchies among all the various indigenous peoples.

Divine revelation is always to be found most clearly in individual realization and nowhere else. Here, in what is often called mysticism, Christianity and the Native American traditions most obviously meet. It is true that divine realization among the Native Americans tends to manifest itself through dreams and visions; yet it is also true that in the Bible we read, "Your old men shall dream dreams, and your young men shall seek visions."[122] If on the one hand the Amerindian traditions often entail spiritual revelation manifested through subtle or psychic images, and if on the other hand Christianity in its primordial form manifests the Great Mysteries laid bare, nonetheless these represent two aspects of the same divine revelation.

Understanding this great mystery at the center of religious revelation, and at the center of Christianity, requires looking toward those who have experienced it. One of the greatest spiritual teachers in all of Christian history was Johannes Tauler, who said that if we are to come to know God, we must "detach ourselves from everything temporal and transitory." We must "cut ourselves off from all those natural pleasures we find most gratifying: society, fashion, . . . [for] it is indeed a wilderness into which God is taking us: a life of detachment in which we shed our desires, spiritual and natural, in our interior and exterior life."[123]

These are the conditions of spirituality in all traditions: one retires from the transitory and seeks the eternal. Spiritual seekers, in any tradition, at some point find themselves leaving behind the gratifications of society and traveling into the spiritual wilderness, leaving behind the world of desires. Certainly this is true in Native American traditions, in which spiritual practice was enjoined on everyone but it is also true in other ways, for one who receives initiation into a spiritual family also must receive that initiation alone—just as the dreamer dreams alone and the visionary sees a vision in solitude.

At the center of all these forms of sacred revelation is the Unknown, which has "neither form nor image nor any other mode nor manner; nor are there any concepts of space." At the center of our being is a divine abyss, in which neither time nor space hold, and which calls us unto its deeps, into its wilderness. Tauler writes:

> No one can imagine the solitude which reigns in this wilderness, no one at all. No thought can enter here, not a word of all the learned treatises . . . Not a single word. So inward is it, so infinitely remote, and so untouched by time and space. This ground is simple and without differentiation, and when one enters here, it will seem as if one has been here from all eternity, and as if united to God, be it only for an instant.[124]

This mysterious inward ground that transcends time and space, and into which not a thought or word can enter, also transcends terms like "Christian" and "Indian." It is the experiential center, the Council Tree, the Axis of all the worlds, the solitary, inward, eternal centrum.

In the various Amerindian tribal traditions, this centrum, the transcendent Origin and Power that surges through all things, manifests itself in the countless spirits of nature, and especially in the Great Spirits. The spiritual center of all things is known as *wakan tanka* among the Sioux, as *kitchi-manitou* among the Ojibway, and by many other names as well. But it is wrong to conceptualize this spiritual power in the modern fashion, for in truth there is a single spiritual energy or Origin, while there are countless manifestations of it. It is not that there is a deity out there somewhere that we can call *wakan tanka*. Rather, the term *wakan tanka* means Great Mystery, and this mystery manifests all around us and in us as well.

Indeed, according to Native American tradition, as in Christian mystical tradition, humanity is not without a divine spark at its own center. To understand how this is so, however, we need to consider a particular Amerindian metaphysics of being. According to Lakota Sioux teaching, there are three supraphysical and concentric aspects of a being. The body is given life by its *woniya*, or life-breath, which corresponds to the vital aspect of the subtle being. When someone dies, it is his *niya* that leaves first; when he enters the *inipi*, or purification lodge, his *niya* is purified. Then there is the *nagi*, or psyche of the being, his "ghost" or "soul" or personality—the total subtle modality of a being. And at the center of a being is the *nagila*, or essence, which corresponds to the "spirit" of Christian tradition. This correspondence is rather close: for just as the Christian concept of Pentecost implies the universal "descent of the spirit," so too the *nagila*, or essence, is affiliated with *takuskanskan*, the *primum mobile* of Sioux tradition, literally "that which moves all things." It is impersonal.

Now the individual being also possesses *sicun*, or spiritual power, which perhaps most closely approximates the Arabic word *baraka*. In Muslim tradition, a great spiritual leader is seen to have much *baraka*, or spiritual power, and irradiates that beneficent power to those around him; they participate in it, their beings are permeated with it, and in a sense they become it. In Lakota tradition, the *nagi*, or subtle totality of a being—a spirit bear, say—reveals itself to a person in a vision and in the revelation transfers *sicun*, or spiritual power, which is grounded or distilled into a particular spirit rock or other sacred object. This object is kept wrapped in a sacred bundle, and its power is revealed during certain ceremonies or times. At those times, the *sicun*, or spiritual power—of the bear spirit, for instance—remanifests itself; the visionary is again one with his or her vision.[125]

This unity of the visionary and the spirit seen in the vision corresponds to the unity of the Christian mystic with Christ: one could say that as the

Great Mystery manifests itself to the individual visionary by way of an intermediary bear spirit, so too in Christianity the mystic becomes one with the Great Mystery of God through the Christ. The fundamental indivisibility between the holy man and the spirit he sees in a vision, and invokes later, cannot be exaggerated: they are one, and on a psychic or subtle level, the holy man actually *becomes* that spirit.

In the same way, as Philip Sherrard has pointed out, the Christological understanding of the Greek Fathers in particular, but of the Western mystics as well, meant the "doctrine of the God-man," a "deification realized through the participation of the human element in the divine"; the human participates in the universal archetype, just as in Platonic terms all particulars participate in their divine Forms.[126] Here we have an almost complete convergence between Christian and Amerindian traditions: in both, the divine archetype reveals the transcendent Origin of humanity. Humans participate in the divine power they witness, and by that witnessing they go through what in Greek Orthodox theology is called *deification.*

There is of necessity a point at which the created and the uncreated meet within the human being, a spiritual essence that illumines the soul, and of which all traditions give testimony. In *essence,* a human being is not merely a rational animal and does not only exist in a temporal, relative sense but is eternal, absolute. This essential eternality or absoluteness is impersonal; it is revealed to us through spiritual intermediaries, our angelic counterparts who in reality are revealing to our subtle or psychic modality its own uncreated essence.

This is not to say, however, that all spirits of nature reveal transcendent truth equally. As a Lakota named Wahacanka Hotun ("Ringing Shield") put it: "There are a great many spirits. They control everything; and they know everything. . . . They can talk with animals and they can make animals talk with men. The spirits go about in the world all the time and they make everything do as they please."[127] But there are spirits that cause misfortune; and any spirit if displeased can bring about disaster for each of us, since spirits are more powerful than human beings. There are greater and lesser spirits, just as there are greater and lesser gifts of the spirit. One spirit may be one's guide to transcendent vision; another may tell whether tomorrow's hunt will be successful.

There was once a time when the whole of Christianity recognized a spiritual hierarchy, an awareness inherited in part from Platonism and in part from the cumulative Gnostic visionary heritage of the tradition as a whole. This spiritual hierarchy ranged from the elementals, spirits and sprites of nature, dwarves and goblins and faeries, upward to the angelic powers, rank upon rank. Protestantism and rationalism for the most part vanquished this older way of seeing the world—though it remained living in some places, as in Celtic lands. But since Platonism tends to create a spiritual renaissance anywhere in the Western world that it can again take root— as once it did in Florence, Italy—and since Christianity both Eastern and Western has such a long and remarkable heritage, including such teachers as Meister Eckhart, Johannes Tauler, and Jan van Ruysbroeck, not to mention more recent mystics like Jakob Böhme and Jane Lead, one cannot in truth say that Christianity seen in its totality is opposed to the kind of spiritual hierarchies and visionary practices found in Amerindian religious traditions.[128]

The curse of modernity is the destruction of religious traditions from without and from within; so we are often left without guides. But if we seek with humility, and allow our religious tradition into which we were born to permeate our lives, can anyone doubt that the spirit which bloweth where it listeth will guide us toward it, that divine compassion will draw us in?

We, for all our arrogance, cannot destroy a celestial landscape that we cannot reach, that we cannot acknowledge. We all stand upon the same sacred earth; we are all living in the kingdom of the spirit. It is our task to realize our place in this kingdom, the spiritual landscape of native America.

6

THE SONGS of SolitudE and SilENCE

Anyone who has spent time alone in the wilderness knows how the civilized world falls away. All those chattering voices surround us, as if unwilling to relinquish their hold, but slowly they disappear, slowly the rhythms and noises of the cities fade, and we are left alone beneath the stars or in the sun, beside the waters and among the trees. We know that this is the restoring of the soul; we know that in the silence and solitude of the wilderness we can find anew our spirit. But our lives are a forgetting of this truth; we live caught in the spiral of daily events, hurried on by the clock, by a barrage of events and appointments and expectations and entertainments. If we are ever to reenter Native America, if we are ever to recognize the spiritual landscape in which we live, we must do so through silence and solitude.

Many people observe—when one mentions the possibility of restoring to humanity a spiritual understanding of the land and a balanced way of life— that this is all very well but that before modern civilization the population of America was so low one could afford to live without damaging the earth.

126

Today, the argument goes, we have hundreds of millions of people on the same land, and going back to a more balanced way of living would inevitably entail the deaths of many millions of people. Our discussion here, however, is not about mass movements. Rather, it is about individual regeneration, and individual regeneration takes place under the auspices of a spiritual guide and tradition, in silence and solitude.

Often overlooked in any discussion of Native America's population before European colonization is the more certain access to solitude in a pristine landscape that would have been available to the seeker. Today it is hard to find a single place on the face of the earth that is not touched by the hand of modern civilization. But before European colonization, such opportunities were omnipresent. One could go out and fast not far from the tribal village and yet be completely surrounded by wilderness, be completely alone. Such solitude is essential for spiritual practice. Spiritual practice can certainly be carried on in places other than wilderness, but nonetheless, in all religious traditions, one goes into retreat in order to purify oneself and to realize the divine.

In every man or woman who represents a religious tradition there is great dignity. You can see this in the way such people carry themselves: their way of walking, their gestures, everything about them is certain and complete. Many European travelers among the Native Americans during the eighteenth and nineteenth centuries recognized this dignity and certainty among the tribespeople they visited. Not only were the tribal peoples generous and, for the most part, physically beautiful, but there was in them a way of acting that comes from nature herself. William Bartram noted this while traveling among the southeastern tribes, and George Catlin observed it too while traveling among the Plains and midwestern tribes.

This hieratic quality in the dress, in the gestures, and in the carriage of the traditional native peoples directly reflects the majesty and presence of nature herself. The garments of the American Indians symbolically reflect their spiritual archetypes: the eagle headress reveals the Sun in human life, for instance, just as the animal and other forms reveal on garments and in other accoutrements the spiritual archetypes they represent. And as Schuon writes,

> The prestige enjoyed by the Indians in the most diverse milieus and countries is explained by the truly fascinating combination of a heroism

both stoic and intrepid and the extraordinary expressiveness of their faces, garments, and implements, without forgetting—from the psychological and spiritual point of view—a priestly and contemplative, and so to speak mythological climate.[129]

In sum, continues Schuon, the Native American "embodies virgin Nature [and] the sense of the sacred."[130]

To don a sacred headdress or to wear sacred clothing and to paint oneself is to manifest the archetypes of which nature is a reflection, and hence one can see in the sacred dancers and singers the dignity and solitude proper to one alone in the wilderness. At a sacred dance, you are as if alone in the wild, even as you are among the tribal people. There is a plaintive quality in all the sacred songs; the songs, even if sung on a grassy knoll in a city, reverberate in the air and remind us of our primordial nature as human beings in a natural world. Every singer and dancer is as if alone in virgin nature.

These forms of dress, ways of moving, songs and dances are all outward signs of inward silence that irradiates through the tradition; this solitude in the wilderness reverberates through all the songs and arts of the native peoples. For in silence and solitude is the ordering of the being, the harmonizing of body, soul, and spirit. As René Guénon has pointed out, silence in earthly terms corresponds to the Unmanifest in metaphysical terms. And as it is from the Unmanifest that all things proceed, so too in human life all actions are an expression of the silence at their center.[131] To go out into the wilderness and to fast alone is to purify the body and soul; it is to bring oneself closer to the Divine Origin at the center of one's own being and of all beings.

To fast alone and in silence is also to separate oneself from the community and from the things of daily life. To go out into the wilderness is to leave behind the realm of passions and desires, to abandon even the sustenance of the body, and to turn inward to the ordering of the soul and the call of the spirit. One leaves behind not only one's food but the outward demands of society as well, the daily conflicts and the requirements of life in the social world. If in a traditional culture clothing and movement and speech are themselves hieratic on an outward level, this is because the people practice spiritually, alone and yet as part of the tribe.

Spiritual practice and realization is at the center of all traditional art and life. Just as the actions of a saint reflect in this world his spiritual knowledge, so too in a traditional culture, the collective spiritual realization of a people is realized in their arts and in their way of life. But always it is the individual spiritual practice that maintains and renews the religious tradition; and individual spiritual practice must always ultimately take place alone and in the most acute silence. Anyone who has been in a place where deep meditative practice or deep prayer is being undertaken knows the pervasive and complete enveloping silence that fills that ambience. This silence is the heart of the tradition; it is the being's return to and realization of the silence that is at the heart of all nature.

To enter into solitude is to enter into a state of unification; it is to turn inward and to center oneself. In this respect, entering solitude is entering also into the unity that is at the center of the natural world; it is entering into the Divine and nonmanifest Origin that Soen Nakagawi Roshi called "endless dimension universal life." This Origin is at once the silence from which all things proceed and the solitary unmoving center of existence. To enter this solitude and this silence is to enter into perfection and plenitude at the very Axis of being; it is to enter into the Absolute, into that which is inconceivable from a merely human perspective.

This is why, when Black Elk described solitary "lamenting" for a vision, the highest form of lamenting he described is silent. When during the night the lamenter gets up and gives homage to the four quarters, he should also be calling out to the Great Spirit. But when in the early morning he goes forth to give homage to the Morning Star, the lamenter should "point his pipe stem toward this sacred star, [and] should ask it for wisdom; this he should pray silently in his heart and not aloud."[132] To point the pipe stem symbolizes the connection between the star and the lamenter; the pipe stem itself signifies the movement of smoke and of spiritual power. The lamenter prays for wisdom silently because wisdom of the Great Spirit Himself is higher than the protecting beings of the four directions; one calls out to the protectors but wisdom itself comes in holy silence.

So too, Black Elk notes that while the solitary lamenter may at times call aloud, he may also call silently, directing his whole will inwardly toward the Great Spirit. In this case, the lamenter will

remain silent with his whole attention directed to the Great Spirit or to one of His Powers. He must always be careful lest distracting thoughts

come to him, yet he must remain alert to recognize any messenger the
Great Spirit may send to him, for these people often come in the form
of an animal, even one as small and as seemingly insignificant as that
of a little ant.[133]

This silence is not merely the absence of words; rather it is the directing
of the attention toward the divine and corresponds to *zazen* in Zen Buddhist
tradition or to the "prayer of the heart" in Christian tradition. The combi-
nation of alertness and spiritual contemplation alluded to by Black Elk is
precisely what one finds also in Zen Buddhism: in meditation, one enters
into a state of *samadhi*, or spiritual absorption. The aftereffect of this absorption is a heightened awareness, a greater attention to the things around
one.

In an extraordinary state of visionary absorption, Black Elk saw the spiritual
essences of the world and the spiritual beings who guard it. He found himself
"standing on the highest mountain of them all, and round about beneath
me was the whole hoop of the world. And while I stood there I saw more
than I can tell and I understood more than I saw; for I was seeing in a sacred
manner the shapes of all things in the spirit. . . . And I saw that it was holy."[134]
After the vision Black Elk, who at this time was only nine years old, found
himself alone on the plain with the spotted eagle,[135] and he came to his
own teepee, in which his own body had lain still for twelve days—and he
awoke and sat up. But the vision's force reverberated throughout the rest
of his life, so that "I did not have to remember these things; they remembered
themselves all these years."[136]

The spiritual landscape that Black Elk saw, he saw in solitary visionary
absorption; he saw his land and his people's divine protectors with the eyes
of the spirit, and he heard with the ears of the spirit what he was told. A
vision of such force is an event of psychic power that reverberates throughout
a person's life— and so it was that later in his life, Black Elk helped his people
sew onto clothing the designs he had seen in a later vision, just as he sang
songs he had been given and danced dances. Out of profound silence and
solitude—out of a transcendence of the ordinary world and of the body—
these things came.

In extraordinary vision Black Elk saw the spiritual archetypes of his land
and his people, and these archetypes remain—precisely because they are
archetypes. Even if nature has been degraded and laid waste, even if the

native peoples have been decimated and their ways deliberately destroyed, the spiritual realm cannot be touched by the hand of humanity. In it the archetypal remains, pristine and full of joy. It is said in Kabbalistic tradition that even if the tradition were lost, it could be reconstituted, because what was once true is always so. The same may be said of the sacred landscape of Native America.

CONCLUSION

On a turbulent Friday evening in April 1991, a tornado was headed directly for the city of Maple Hill, Kansas, a little town just west of Topeka. A powerful tornado, it had just destroyed a number of buildings and was moving directly for the village when, as the local newspaper reported, "*Buffalo Mound, a hill just west of the town, diverted the twister to the north.*" "It was on the ground within a quarter mile of the town," volunteer fireman Jim Puff said. "We were just awful lucky."[137] One could call it luck. Or one might take into account that Buffalo Mound, the highest point for many miles, was also sacred to the Indian tribes and was a site to which one went for fasting and praying. Is it impossible that such a place might well protect people?

Conversely, however, if a sacred place can protect people, a defiled place may not protect people in the same way. Another tornado roared down upon the city of Topeka, Kansas, in June 1966, narrowly missing the state capitol building, destroying much of the city's university, and leaving devastation in its wake. It was the first tornado in recorded history to strike the area where the city had been built, and it came from directly over a sacred high place above the city to the southwest called Burnett's Mound, or Shunganunga Bluff. This story becomes emblematic when one considers that the city built a huge water tank in that hillside in the preceding years, destroying the ambience of that place.

To dig into this bluff and to destroy part of this sacred place—from which one can see forty miles, the whole horizon spread out in a great circle—surely would anger the spirits. The high Shunganunga Bluff overlooks the entire city of Topeka and forms the head of a long, curving ridge running south, then around toward the east. That this is a sacred place is without question; one is lifted toward the very stars here by the sacred rocks that are extruded over the entire ridge and that make the very top of the mound—save for a single tree—bare of most vegetation.

A sacred high place, where for ages people have gone to fast and be alone with the spirits—a point at which above and below meet—must not be dug into and damaged, for it is charged with spiritual power. When a sacred place is desecrated—which is what the great disklike water tank gouged in the side of the hill entails—one can expect that there will be consequences. One can feel the disturbed energy in the air around the water tower; there is wild graffiti completely encircling the tank, and everywhere around that bluff one feels the sense of desecration.

Many city people know the legend that Shunganunga Bluff protects the city from tornados. Yet virtually everyone will scoff at such "superstitions." In a very real sense this legend *is* a superstition—for it is the residue of the truth that the bluff irradiates a spiritual presence derived at once from its nature as a high place and from its significance as a sacred site, a place where heaven and earth meet. Too often we moderns have only a dim awareness—like a light shining under a door we have closed—that our relation to the spiritual is far more important than our use of the bluff for practical purposes. Sometimes we express this dim awareness in legends, the significance of which we no longer grasp. But the legends can still be operative.

High places are revered in all the world's religions. Christ went to the mountain to pray; Hindu and Buddhist ascetics have long gone to the sacred mountains to practice; there are sacred mountains in Islam, in Judaism, in Taoism, and in aboriginal religious traditions. The sacred mountain is a place for isolation, prayer, and fasting, and it also irradiates its spiritual influence over the world. The mountain or high place—the place of spiritual exertion—emanates spiritual protection. This is a great mystery, the spiritual significance of the sacred mountains, each of which body forth the Mountain at the center of which is the Axis of our cosmos.

On a mountain, one is symbolically above the things of this world, above the hubbub of desire, anger, and folly. One is closer to the Origin and to the heavens. This is the meaning of the sacred retreat to the mountains of the Native Americans as well—but a bluff like Shunganunga can represent the same significance for us. Just as a great mountain like Mount Kailas in the Himalayas has spiritual significance for the whole world, so too a high place like Shunganunga has meaning for its locale. The principle remains the same. If one not only ignores this truth, but actually goes so far as to intentionally damage such a sacred place, is it so surprising that there will be negative consequences—just as when one goes on a holy pilgrimage to a sacred site, there are positive consequences?

These rather dramatic instances of the tornados and the high places illustrate clearly two ways of looking at nature and the human place in the world. One the one hand, one can recognize that the long serpentine ridge and the high peak on its end—from which one can see forty miles on a good day—is holy ground, and that on its height, with spiritual exertion, may come the great gift of spiritual revelation that will illuminate one's being and fill one's life with gratitude and joy. On the other hand, one may disregard the spiritual significance of life on earth and regard the bluff merely as a place that, gouged out on one side, will hold a water tank more cheaply than a tower. The first view is one of spiritual richness; the second is one of spiritual poverty, of materialist emptiness.

Naturally, Shunganunga Bluff is not the only place in America that exemplifies what results from modern ignorance of and destruction of the sacred. There are countless other desecrated places in America; there are other cities that have experienced tornados or other kinds of destruction under similar circumstances—and indeed, our "environmental crisis" seen *in toto* directly results from modern blindness of the same kind as that which caused the city to gouge out the bluff for a water storage tank. When calculating our economic or political costs and benefits, we must consider above all the spiritual costs and benefits of what we do, for those costs and benefits have repercussions in all aspects of our lives—and afterlives.

Modern environmentalists occasionally use Native American religious traditions to justify the preservation of "biosystems." Yet from the perspective of any traditional religion, what matters is not only the preservation of the natural world and of sacred sites for their own sake, but the preservation of those sites and wild places because of their spiritual significance. Christ retired to the wilderness; Siddhartha retired to the wilderness; Amerindians have gone into spiritual retreat in the wilderness for uncounted ages. Under the auspices of authentic religious tradition and its representative in the holy man, one learns to open oneself to the spiritual meaning of the human place in this natural world.

We each must come to terms with who we are as spiritual beings and with the natural world as a place of spiritual revelation. This is particularly true in America, where there is so little concern for the preservation of open land, where unlike Europe so far, cities are allowed to sprawl over the countryside endlessly, eating up the earth and leaving behind gaudy, tawdry, garish, decaying commercial strips and rows of rotting apartments. American mercantilism is omnivorous and will not stop until it has consumed everything beautiful; it seems altogether evident that one cannot stop the juggernaut of the modern world. But each individual can come to understand spiritual truth, can see the world in a new way, and can become spiritually renewed, regenerated.

We moderns believe so fervently in illusions of "progress" or "evolution" that we have blinded ourselves to our true situation on this earth. We believe that the warnings of a Jeremiah against ignoring spiritual truth belong to the past, that we can overcome through technology the very evils we create daily. Yet countless civilizations have fallen before ours, and it is to be expected that our own era too is but a brief crescendo, a short, noisy, chaotic moment in the great gyres of time. It is doubtful that we can turn this moment of decay backward, that we can reverse the avalanche of modernity that sweeps away all things we love. But we can turn toward that which is undying, toward the celestial landscape that is spread out about us if we could only see it.

Years of modern civilization's destructive power have left many Native American traditions in a perilous state. In some cases, entire tribes have been obliterated; in other cases, the lineage of holy men has ended, so that the young who seek spiritual truth must do so without guidance or protection; and in still other cases, all the elements of the tradition still exist but have been forced underground. In all cases, the skepticism, materialism, and sheer antireligiosity of the modern world erodes what remains of tribal spirituality. Indeed, it often appears—as it did to William Bartram, who traveled among the noble, generous Muscolgulges, Choctaws, Chickasaws, and Cherokees of southeastern America during the eighteenth century—that "vast armies of these evil spirits have invaded this continent, and closely invested them [the tribal peoples] on all sides." While it seems "natural, eligible, and even easy, for these simple, illiterate people to put in practice those beautiful lectures delivered to us by the ancient sages and philosophers . . . we behold the ill, immoral conduct of too many white people, who reside amongst them."[138]

One cannot but be ashamed after considering the European-American history of "Indian hating"—it is a history of unparalleled abuse and perfidy. Yet that history cannot be changed, and what matters today is, on the one hand, the preservation of those Amerindian traditions that still remain, so that the tribes may maintain their spiritual practices, and on the other hand, recognition of those traditions' importance to other religious traditions. Judeo-Christian, Buddhist, Muslim—those who practice these religions in America need to learn from the Native American traditions. These world religions need to become acclimated in North America; for them to truly take root and flourish, they must become grounded in American sacred earth.

When we look at world religious history, we see that in every case, when a religious tradition enters a new land, it takes within itself the existing native religious traditions. When Christianity invaded northern Europe and Ireland, for example, it opposed many of the native traditions (the noble indigenous spirituality was represented as evil—as was that of the Amerindians), but eventually Christianity assimilated aspects of the indigenous religions. Churches were built on ground known as sacred long before the invaders themselves arrived on the spot; spiritual practices and symbols in the Church took on aspects of indigenous spirituality. Indeed, before long one had in Ireland, for example, Celtic Christianity.

Likewise, when the Buddhadharma came to Tibet, one saw Tibetan Buddhism overcome the Bön religion and assimilate many of its traditions and sacred sites into the Buddhist tradition. Tibetan Buddhism differs in many ways from Indian Buddhism, Chinese Buddhism, or Japanese Buddhism, not to mention the many schools and other divisions of this vast and rich religious tradition, and each of these schools and traditions expresses a particular manifestation of Buddhism as a whole. In each case, Buddhism came to express the already existent religious nature of the land and people where it took root.

So too, we in America who follow an "imported" spiritual path need to recognize the autochthonous spiritual traditions that have existed long before our own much-trumpeted arrival. We need to realize that there are sacred sites in the Americas just as there are sacred sites in the Middle East, in Asia, in Europe, and in Australia—indeed, everywhere that there are authentic spiritual traditions. Not only are there sacred sites here, but there is a particular kind of spiritual practice in a sense indigenous to the land itself. The unity found within the diversity of Amerindian religious traditions is not mere chance, and any spiritual tradition worthy of the name must entail an awareness of and an openness to the indigenous spirituality that manifests in the Amerindian traditions.

APPENDIX

In 1988, the United States Supreme Court decided—in the case of Lyng v. Northwest Indian Cemetery Protective Association *(1988) 485 US 439; 99L Ed 2d 534; 108 S Ct 1319—that despite the constitutional right to freedom of religious practice in the United States, and despite the absence of any compelling economic or social necessity, the United States Forest Service had the right to put a road through a Native American sacred place and could lumber forest land that had been sacred to tribal people for genera-tions. In brief, the Supreme Court supported the destruction of a sacred landscape and of the religious practices of Native people in that area. This decision is one in a series of decisions that continue to erode religious freedom in the United States. What follows are excerpts from the eloquent dissenting opinion of Justice William Brennan, joined by Justices Thurgood Marshall and Harry A. Blackmun, on this unfortunate case. To increase readability, some legal references have been omitted.*

For at least 200 years and probably much longer, the Yurok, Karok, and Tolowa Indians have held sacred an approximately 25-square-mile area of land situated in what is today the Blue Creek Unit of Six Rivers National Forest in northwestern California. As the Government readily concedes, regular visits to this area, known to respondent Indians as the "high country," have played and continue to play a "critical" role in the religious practices and rituals of these tribes. . . . These beliefs, only briefly described in the Court's opinion, are crucial to a proper understanding to the respondents' claims.

As the Forest Service's commissioned study, the Theodoratus Report, explains, for Native Americans religion is not a discrete sphere of activity separate from all others, and any attempt to isolate the religious aspects of Indian life "is in reality an exercise which forces Indian concepts into non-Indian categories." Thus, for most Native Americans, "the area of worship cannot be delineated from social, political, cultur[al], and other areas o[f] Indian lifestyle" (statement of Barney Old Coyote, Crow tribe). A pervasive feature of this lifestyle is the individual's relationship with the natural world; this relationship, which can accurately though somewhat incompletely be characterized as one of stewardship, forms the core of what might be called, for want of a better nomenclature, the Indian religious experience. While traditional western religions view creation as the work of a deity "who institutes natural laws which then govern the operation of physical nature," tribal religions regard creation as an ongoing process in which they are morally and religiously obligated to participate. Native Americans fulfill this duty through ceremonies and rituals designed to preserve and stabilize the earth and to protect humankind from disease and other catastrophes. Failure to conduct these ceremonies in the manner and place specified, adherents believe, will result in great harm to the earth and to the people whose welfare depends upon it.

In marked contrast to traditional western religions, the belief systems of Native Americans do not rely on doctrines, creeds, or dogmas. Established or universal truths—the mainstay of western religions—play no part in Indian faith. Ceremonies are communal efforts undertaken for specific purposes in accordance with instructions handed down from generation to generation. . . . Where dogma lies at the heart of western religions, Native American faith is inexorably bound to the use of land. The site-specific nature of Indian religious practice derives from the Native American perception that land is itself a sacred, living being. Rituals are performed in prescribed locations not merely as a matter of traditional orthodoxy, but because land, like all other living things, is unique, and specific sites possess different spiritual properties and significance. Within this belief system, therefore, land is not fungible; indeed, at the time of the Spanish colonization of the American southwest, "all . . . Indians held in some form a belief in a sacred and indissoluble bond between themselves and the land in which their settlements were located." E. Spicer, *Cycles of Conquest: The Impact of Spain, Mexico, and the United States on the Indians of the Southwest 1533–1960,* p. 576 (1962).

For respondent Indians, the most sacred of lands is the high country where, they believe, prehuman spirits moved with the coming of humans to the earth. Because these spirits are seen as the source of religious power, or "medicine," many of the tribes' rituals and practices require frequent journeys to the area. Thus, for example, religious leaders preparing for the complex of ceremonies that underlie the tribes' World Renewal efforts must travel to specific sites in the high country in order to attain the medicine necessary for successful renewal. Similarly, individual tribe members may seek curative powers for the healing of the sick, or personal medicine for particular purposes such as good luck in singing, hunting, or love. A period of preparation generally precedes such visits, and individuals must select trails in the sacred area according to the medicine they seek and their abilities, gradually moving to increasingly more powerful sites, which are typically located at higher altitudes. Among the most powerful of sites are Chimney Rock, Doctor Rock, and Peak 8, all of which are elevated rock outcroppings.

According to the Theodoratus Report, the qualities "of silence, the aesthetic perspective, and the physical attributes, are an extension of the sacrednes of [each] particular site." The act of medicine making is akin to meditation: the individual must integrate physical, mental, and vocal actions in order to communicate with the prehuman spirits. As a result, "successful use of the high country is dependent upon and facilitated by certain qualities of the physical environment, the most important of which are privacy, silence, and an undisturbed natural setting." Although few tribe members actually make medicine at the most powerful sites, the entire tribe's welfare hinges on the success of the individual practitioners.

Beginning in 1972, the Forest Service began preparing a multiple-use management plan for the Blue Creek Unit. The plan's principal features included the harvesting of 733 million board feet of Douglas fir over an 80-year period, and the completion of a six-mile segment of paved road (the G-O road). The road's primary purpose was to provide a route for hauling the timber harvested under the management plan; in addition, it would enhance public access to the Six Rivers and other national forests, and allow for more efficient maintenance and fire control by the Forest Service itself. In the mid-1970's, the Forest Service circulated draft environmental impact statements evaluating the effects of several proposed routes for the final segment of the G-O road, including at least two that circumnavigated the high country altogether. Ultimately, however, the Service settled on a route running along the Chimney Rock Corridor, which traverses the Indians' sacred lands.

Respondent Indians brought suit to enjoin implementation of the plan, alleging that the road construction and timber harvesting would impermissibly interfere with their religious practices in violation of the Free Exercise Clause of the First Amendment. Following a trial, the District Court granted the requested injunctive relief. The court found that "use of the high country is essential to [respondents'] 'World Renewal' ceremonies . . . which constitute the heart of the Northwest Indian religious belief system," and that "intrusions on the sanctity of the Blue Creek high country are . . . potentially destructive of the very core of Northwest [Indian] religious beliefs and practices. Concluding that these burdens on respondent's religious practices were sufficient to trigger the protections of the Free Exercise Clause, the court found that the interests served by the G-O road and the management plan were insufficient to justify those burdens. In particular, the court found that the road would not improve access to the timber resources in the Blue Creek Unit and indeed was unnecessary to the harvesting of that timber; that it would not significantly improve the administration of the Six Rivers National Forest; and that it would increase recreational access only marginally, and at the expense of the very pristine environment that makes the area suitable for primitive recreational use in the first place.

[Likewise, the Ninth Circuit Court of Appeals found in the respondents' favor, and] affirmed the District Court's determination that the proposed harvesting and construction activities violated respondents' constitutional rights. Recognizing that the high country is "indispensable" to the religious lives of the approximately 5000 tribe members who reside in the area, the court concluded "that the proposed government operations would *virtually destroy the . . . Indians' ability to practice their religion.*" Like the lower court, the Court of Appeals found the Government's interest in building the road and permitting limited timber harvesting— interests which of course were considerably undermined by the passage of the California Wilderness Act—did not justify the destruction of respondents' religion.

The [Supreme] Court does not for a moment suggest that the interests served by the G-O road are in any way compelling, or that they outweigh the destructive effect construction of the road will have on respondents' religious practices. Instead, the Court embraces the Government's contention that its prerogative as landowner should always take precedence over a claim that a particular use of federal property infringes religious practices. Attempting to justify this rule, the Court argues that the First Amendment bars only outright prohibitions, indirect coercion, and penalties on the free exercise of religion. . . .

[But] I . . . cannot accept the Court's premise that the form of the Government's restraint on religious practice, rather than its effect, controls our constitutional analysis. Respondents here have demonstrated that completion of the G-O road will completely frustrate the practice of their religion, for as the lower courts have found, the proposed logging and construction activities will virtually destroy respondents' religion, and will therefore necesarily force them into abandoning those practices altogether. Indeed, the Government's proposed activities will restrain religious practice to a far greater degree here than in any of the cases cited by the Court today. None of the religious adherents in *Hobbie, Thomas,* and *Sherbert,* for example, claimed or could have claimed that the denial of unemployment benefits rendered the practice of their religions impossible; at most, the challenged laws made those practices more expensive. Here, in stark contrast, respondents have claimed—and proved—that the desecration of the high country will prevent religious leaders from attaining the religious power or medicine indispensable to the success of virtually all their rituals and ceremonies. . . .

The Court's distinction [does] not comport with the principles animating the constitutional guarantee: religious freedom is threatened no less by governmental action that makes the practice of one's chosen faith impossible than by governmental programs that pressure one to engage in conduct inconsistent with religious beliefs. The Court attempts to explain the line it draws by arguing that the protections of the Free Exercise Clause "cannot depend on measuring the effects of a governmental action on a religious objector's spiritual development." . . . While I agree that governmental action that simply offends religious sensibilities may not be challenged under the clause, we have recognized that laws that affect spiritual development by impeding the integration of children into the religious community or by increasing the expense of adherence to religious principles—in short, laws that frustrate or inhibit religious practice—trigger the protections of the constitutional guarantee.

Both common sense and our prior cases teach us, therefore, that governmental action that makes the practice of a given faith more difficult necessarily penalizes that practice and thereby tends to prevent adherence to religious belief. The harm to the practitioners is the same regardless of the manner in which the Government restrains their religious expression, and the Court's fear that an "effects" test will permit religious adherents to challenge governmental actions they merely find "offensive" in no way justifies its refusal to recognize the constitutional injury citizens suffer when governmental action not only offends but actually restrains their religious practices. Here, respondents have demonstrated that the Government's proposed activities will completely prevent them from practicing their religion, and such a showing . . . entitles them to the protections of the Free Exercise Clause. . . . That [the Court's] reading is wholly untenable . . . is demonstrated by the cruelly surreal result it produces here: governmental action that will virtually destroy a religion is nevertheless deemed not to "burden" that religion. . . .

Today's ruling sacrifices a religion at least as old as the Nation itself, along with the spiritual well-being of its approximately 5000 adherents, so that the Forest Service can build a six-mile segment of road that two lower courts found had only the most marginal and speculative utility, both to the government itself and to the private lumber interests that might conceivably use it. . . . Today, the Court holds that a federal land-use decision that promises to destroy an entire religion does not burden the practice of that faith in the manner recognized by the Free Exercise [of Religion] Clause. Having thus stripped respondents and all other Native Americans of any constitutional protection against perhaps the most serious threat to their age-old practices, and indeed to their entire way of life, the Court assures us that nothing in its decision "should be read to encourage governmental insensitivity to the religious needs of any citizen."

I find it difficult . . . to imagine conduct more insensitive to religious needs than the Government's determination to build a marginally useful road in the face of uncontradicted evidence that the road will render the practice of respondents' religion impossible. Nor do I believe that respondents will derive any solace from the knowledge that although the practice of their religion will become "more difficult" as a result of the Government's actions, they remain free to maintain their religious beliefs. Given today's ruling, that freedom amounts to nothing more than the right to believe that their religion will be destroyed. The safeguarding of such a hollow freedom not only makes a mockery of the "policy of the United States to protect and preserve for American Indians their inherent right of freedom to believe, express, and exercise the[ir] traditional religions," it fails utterly to accord with the dictates of the First Amendment.

I dissent.

NOTES

1. John Collier, *The Indians of the Americas* (New York: Norton, 1947), pp. 15–17.

2. As Philip Sherrard has eloquently written: "Modern science has its origin in a loss of memory, a forgetfulness by man of who he is. . . . Progressively divorced by his ignorance from the roots of his being, man, so long as he persists in this course, is doomed to advance blindly and at an ever-increasing pace towards total loss of identity, total loss of control, and eventually to total self-destruction. Nothing can stop this process except a complete reversal of direction. And nothing can initiate a reversal of direction except a recovery by man of an awareness of who he is: the cure must go back to where the sickness started." Quoted from *The Eclipse of Man and Nature* (London: Golgonooza, 1987), pp. 88–89.

3. This is the absurd evolutionist doctrine that finds its semifinal, laughable form in Teilhard de Chardin's attempts to clothe the majesty of Christianity with evolutionism. In his work we see how evolutionism is ultimately an antireligious attempt at what amounts to a secular mythology. This desire to irreligiously merge religion and science drove Teilhard to the length of writing a paean to nuclear war as the apotheosis of humankind. See Seyyed Hossein Nasr, *Knowledge and the Sacred* (New York: Crossroad, 1981), pp. 240–244 on Teilhardism.

4. Seyyed Hossein Nasr, *Man and Nature: The Spiritual Crisis of Modern Man* (Kuala Lumpur, Malaysia: Foundation for Traditional Studies, 1976), p. 21.

5. See in this regard the works of John Michell on the British sacred stones.

6. See James R. Walker, *Lakota Ritual and Belief* (Lincoln, Nebr.: University of Nebraska Press, 1980), pp. 72–73.

7. Walker, p. 208.

8. Walker, pp. 96–98.

9. Walker, p. 118.

10. On the secularization of time, see Nasr (1981), pp. 227–229.

11. The Sacred Cow is said to live in the Golden Age on four legs, in the Silver on three, in the Bronze on two, and in the Final Age on one leg. The symbolism— 4, 3, 2, 1—corresponds to the Pythagorean symbol of the *tetraktys:*

```
         *  *  *  *
          *  *  *
           *  *
            *
```

12. This description of Hopi tradition is derived in part from Frank Waters, *Book of the Hopi* (New York: Penguin, 1982). Unfortunately, here and elsewhere in his writings, Waters succumbs to an evolutionist interpretation of Hopi religion that is as unwarranted as a Marxist or any other anachronistic Western misreading of traditional doctrines. There can be no median point between scientistic dogma and religious tradition; they are fundamentally and irrevocably opposed, for science is rooted in the denial of spirituality or the transcendent.

13. Walker, pp. 76–77.

14. According to Crashing Thunder, the Winnebago counseled their young by saying: "Not with the blessing of one spirit, not with the blessing of twenty spirits, can you go on the war-path. You shall be blessed by all the spirits there are on the earth, those that are pinned through the earth (the Earth-weights), and those underneath the earth; by all these, and by all those in the waters, and all those on the sides of the earth (the Winds); and by the Sun, the Moon, the Day, the Earth." See Paul Radin, ed., *Crashing Thunder: The Autobiography of an American Indian* (New York: Appleton, 1926), p. 452.

15. Jones, *Notes on the Fox Indians,* p. 216.

16. There are disruptions of the fundamental law against one species breeding with or turning into another: lycanthropy and other theriomorphic transformations fall into this category. But in general such transformations are regarded with fear or loathing. Evolutionary theory, which *depends* upon precisely such a transformation from one species into another, is from a traditional Amerindian, Platonic, Buddhist, Hindu, Muslim, Christian, or Judaic viewpoint, utterly absurd.

17. Charles Eastman, *The Soul of the Indian* (Boston: Houghton, 1911), pp. 76–77.

18. In the Sioux world there are three forms of medicine or healing. There is *payjayhutah,* literally "root," which refers to herbal medicine. Then there is the more general term *wapiya,* "which literally means readjusting or making anew." Then there is *wakan,* which "signifies spirit of mystery." See Eastman, pp. 74–75. These three levels of healing correspond to the three worlds: physical, subtle, and celestial.

19. The vision quest as such occurs less frequently, or not at all, among the Amerindians of the Southwest and in Mexico; there, one is said to have the *nagual* from birth. Whether one goes out alone and seeks a vision or gains spiritual revelation through ceremonial mediation is in this sense irrelevant: everyone in the tradition participates in spiritual reality.

20. See Frank Speck, *A Study of the Delaware Indian Big House Ceremony,* vol. 2 (1931; publication of the Pennsylvania Historical Commission), pp. 80–85; see also Elizabeth Tooker, ed., *Native North American Spirituality of the Eastern Woodlands* (New York: Paulist Press, 1979), pp. 105–106.

21. See Gene Weltfish, *The Lost Universe: Pawnee Life and Culture* (Lincoln, Nebr.: University of Nebraska Press, 1965), chap. 12, pp. 124ff.

22. The Pawnee also had a Corn Ceremony for the horticultural aspect of the tribe's life; this ceremony too was inaugurated by a visionary, who had to stay in a sacred robe while the corn ripened, as its incarnate protector.

23. See Ake Hultkranz, *Belief and Worship in Native North America* (Syracuse, N.Y.: Syracuse University Press, 1981), pp. 151–152. Hultkranz discusses the Shoshoni, but the same is true across the continent. After two centuries of persecution, however, such traditions are rarely spoken of to whites.

24. Theanthropic or universal man is also found within Muslim and Judaic traditions; in both he is figured in an Adamic context. See 'Abd Al-Karim Al-Jili, *Universal Man,* translated by Titus Burckhardt (Sherborne, England: Beshara, 1983); on Adam Kadmon (a principal figure in the Jewish esoteric tradition), see Leo Schaya, *The Universal Meaning of the Kabbalah* (London: Allen and Unwin, 1973), especially pp. 82–83.

25. See Arthur Versluis, "In the Tracks of the Buddha: The Footprint Image and Its Meanings," in *Avaloka: A Journal of Traditional Religion and Culture,* 1, no. 2 (1987), pp. 17ff. One finds footprint images on stones in Kansas, incidentally—just as in Buddhist holy sites in Asia.

26. Both Buddhism and Amerindian traditions—like all traditional religions—recognize that history consists of a primordial revelation and its successive decadence or erosion over time. In Buddhist scriptures these ages of progressive decadence are clearly outlined. In Hinduism and Lakota Sioux traditions, this truth is represented in the form of a sacred cow or bull, who stands first on four, then on three, then on two, and finally on one leg as the primordial revelation is lost. See in this regard Joseph Epes Brown, ed., *The Sacred Pipe* (New York: Penguin, 1972), pp. 9, 100; on the traditional understanding of our era and of time, see René Guénon, *The Reign of Quantity* (London: Luzac, 1953), passim.

27. Brown, ed., pp. 45–46.

28. This is how Ohiyesa described the visionary quest: "That solitary communion with the Unseen which was the highest expression of our religious life is partly described in the word *hambeday,* literally 'mysterious feeling,' which has been variously translated 'fasting' and 'dreaming.' It may better be interpreted as 'consciousness of the divine.'

"The first *hambeday,* or religious retreat, marked an epoch in the life of the youth, which may be compared to that of confirmation or conversion in Christian experience. Having first prepared himself by means of the purifying vapor-bath, and cast off as far as possible all human or fleshy influences, the young man sought out the noblest height, the most commanding summit in all the surrounding region. Knowing that God sets no value upon material things, he took with him no offerings or sacrifices other than symbolic objects, such as paints and tobacco. Wishing to appear before Him in all humility, he wore no clothing save his moccasins and breech-clout. At the solemn hour of sunrise or sunset he took up his position, overlooking the glories of earth and facing the 'Great Mystery,' and there he remained, naked, erect, silent, and motionless, exposed to the elements and forces of His arming, for a night and a day to two days and nights, but rarely longer.

"When he returned to the camp, he . . . remain[ed] at a distance until he had again entered the vapor-bath and prepared himself for the intercourse with his fellows. Of the vision or sign vouchsafed to him he did not speak, unless it had included some commission which must be publicly fulfilled."

Generally, Eastman's account, from *The Soul of the Indian,* pp. 7–9, is not wrong, although it is at times romanticized and contains some relatively minor inaccuracies.

29. See Brown, ed., *The Sacred Pipe,* pp. 31ff.; see too Arval Looking Horse, "The Sacred Pipe in Modern Life," in R. J. DeMallie and D. R. Parks, eds., *Sioux Indian Religion* (Norman, Okla.: University of Oklahoma Press, 1987), pp. 67ff.

30. There are many connections between Zen Buddhist and Amerindian traditions. Some roshis have traveled to Native American sacred sites and sat in meditation there; others have presided over the building of monasteries in the mountains and speak of the "mountain deity" and of the spiritual presences there. Both traditions, needless to say, are deeply attuned to the spirituality of the natural world, and for this reason among others we will draw on Rinzai Zen Buddhism in the following discussion.

31. Compare the passage from the Bible (Mark 10:14): "Unless ye become as these little ones, ye cannot enter the kingdom of heaven."

According to Eastman (Ohiyesa), "The original attitude of the American Indian toward the Eternal, the 'Great Mystery' that surrounds and embraces us, was as simple as it was exalted. To him it was the supreme conception, bringing with it the fullest measure of joy and satisfaction possible in this life. The worship of the 'Great Mystery' was silent, solitary, free from all self-seeking. It was silent, because all speech is of necessity feeble and imperfect. . . . It was solitary, because they believed that He is nearer to us in solitude, and there were no priests authorized to come between a man and his Maker. None might exhort or confess or in any way meddle with the religious experience of another." From *The Soul of the Indian,* p. 4.

32. Black Elk said that during one of his vision quests, "On one of the nights the bad spirits came and started tearing the offerings off the poles; and I heard their voices under the ground and one of them said: 'Go and see if he is crying.' And

I heard rattles, but all the time they were outside the sacred place and could not get in, for I had resolved not to be afraid, and did not stop sending my voice to Wakan-Tanka for aid. . . . I was well prepared, you see, and did not weaken, and so nothing bad could happen." Brown, ed., p. 60.

33. Eastman says, "There were no temples or shrines among us save those of nature. Being a natural man, the Indian was intensely poetical. He who enrobes Himself in filmy veils of cloud, there on the rim of the visible world where our Great-Grandfather Sun kindles his evening camp-fire, He who rides upon the rigorous wind of the north, or breathes forth His spirit upon aromatic southern airs, . . . He needs no lesser cathedral," pp. 5–6.

34. Antonio de Herrera wrote that "the Devil deluded them, appearing in the shape of a lion, or a tiger, or a coyote, a beast like a wolf, or in the shape of an alligator, a snake, or a bird, which they called *naguales,* signifying keepers or guardians. . . . The manner of contracting this alliance was thus: the Indian repaired to the river, wood, hill, or most obscure place, where he called upon the devils by such names as he thought fit, talked to the rivers, rocks, or woods, said he went to weep that he might have the same his predecessors had, carrying a cock or dog to sacrifice. In that melancholy fit he fell asleep, and either in a dream or waking, saw some one of the aforesaid birds or other creatures, whom he entreated to grant him profit in salt, cacao, or any other commodity, making his contract at the same time with the said creature, the which, either in a dream or waking, told him, 'Such a day, you shall go abroad a-sporting, and I will be the first bird or other animal you shall meet, and will be your *nagual* and companion at all times.' In *General History of the Continent and Islands of America,* translated by John Stevens (London: 1726), p. 138.

35. See Johann Georg Kohl, *Kitchi-Gami: Life Among the Lake Superior Ojibway,* translated by L. Wraxall (1860; reprint; St. Paul, Minn.: Minnesota Historical Society Press, 1985), pp. 207–208.

36. See Peter Matthiessen's garrulous *Indian Country* (New York: Viking, 1982), a sad, a damning account of modern America's "New Indian Wars." Persecution of the original peoples has not ceased by any means; a culture that universally manifests spirituality cannot be abided by a debased, greed-driven, rapacious modern world. There is today a spiritual battle; it has always been a spiritual battle, and the whites, for the most part, have bodied forth evil. One can massacre a people by building a Tellico Dam over their sacred native land just as much as, and perhaps more effectively than, by shooting them.

37. Ohiyesa wrote: "It is my personal belief, after thirty-five years' experience of it, that there is no such thing as 'Christian civilization.' I believe that Christianity and modern civilization are opposed and irreconcilable, and that the spirit of Christianity and of our ancient religion is essentially the same." Eastman, p. 24. In a fundamental sense, this is true—but it is also true that Christian missionaries have acted to destroy other religious traditions all around the world, as the "missionaries" not of religion but of "civilization" alone.

38. See Waters, p. 24.

39. Frances Densmore, *Teton Sioux Music, Smithsonian Bulletin,* 61 (1918), p. 214.

40. Arthur Amiotte, "The Lakota Sun Dance," in DeMallie and Parks, eds., p. 86.

41. Clark Mallam, *Site of the Serpent, A Prehistoric Life Metaphor in South Central Kansas* (Lyons, Kansas: Coronado-Quivira Museum No. 1), p. 23.

42. Like the *naga* in Buddhist tradition, the Great Horned Snakes in Amerindian tradition are affiliated with skin diseases and with a kind of possession. On *nagas* in Buddhist tradition, see Terry Clifford, *Tibetan Buddhist Medicine* (New York: Weiser, 1986).

43. One could also rely upon Zuñi tradition regarding the *kolowsi,* that peoples' name for the Great Horned Serpents whose places are holy springs and watercourses. Fundamentally, again, Amerindian traditions are unitary.

44. On the shamanism of the *jossakid* and the shaking tent see Kohl, pp. 244–245; the Ojibway knew that the Europeans had landed in America and actually traveled eastward to meet them.

45. G. Weltfish, pp. 274, 316–317.

46. See Werner Müller, *Pre-Columbian American Religions,* translated by S. Davis (London: Weidenfeld, 1968), p. 170; see also Leo Simmons, *Sun Chief: The Autobiography of a Hopi Indian* (New Haven, Conn.: Yale University Press, 1970), p. 17.

47. See James Murie, *Ceremonies of the Pawnee,* vol. 1 (Washington, D.C.: Smithsonian Inst., 1981), pp. 38–39.

48. See Kohl, pp. 215, 218–219. This paradise is without war or strife, and in it is luminescent food, compared by Kohl's Ojibway acquaintances to phosphorescent mushrooms.

49. See Ake Hultkranz, *Native Religions of North America* (New York: Harper & Row, 1987), p. 49.

50. See Alanson Skinner, "Social Life and Ceremonial Bundles of the Menominee Indians," in *Anthropological Papers of the American Museum of Natural History,* 13, no. 1 (1913), pp. 182–183.

51. Skinner, pp. 82–83.

52. See note 51 above.

53. This corresponds to the Kabbalistic doctrine of the *qlipoth,* or "residue of creation," on which see Gerschom Scholem, *Kabbalah* (Jerusalem: Keter, 1974), pp. 138–139; see also Schaya, pp. 110–111, on the "lower world" of *tohu.*

54. See James Murie, "Pawnee Societies," in *Anthropological Papers of the American Museum of Natural History,* 11 (1915), pp. 580–581.

55. See Robert Lowie, "Arikara Societies," in *Anthropological Papers of the American Museum of Natural History,* 11 (1915), pp. 674–675.

56. John C. Neihardt, ed., *Black Elk Speaks* (1932; reprint; New York: Pocket, 1972), chap. 16, "Heyoka Ceremony."

57. See also Thoman Tynon, "The *Wakinyan* Are *Wakan,"* in DeMallie and Parks, eds., pp. 155–157.

58. One rule among the "Contraries," according to the Cheyenne, was that they not touch metal implements or dinnerware. See George Bird Grinnell, *The Cheyenne Indians: Their History and Ways of Life,* vol. 2 (New York: Cooper, 1962), p. 120. This corresponds to a prohibition more generally against wearing metal into any sacred ceremony—a prohibition common not only among the Native Americans but around the world.

59. See Frithjof Schuon, *The Feathered Sun: Plains Indians in Art and Philosophy* (Bloomington, Ind.: World Wisdom, 1990), p. 88.

60. See, for instance, Clyde Kluckhohn, *Navaho Witchcraft* (Boston: Beacon Press, 1944), passim. Witchcraft was reported among the eastern Woodland tribes almost immediately upon white contact; in proportion as tribal traditions were destroyed by the whites, individualistic or egotistic tendencies manifested among the tribes as sorcery or black magic—which is essentially the inverted use of traditional or authentic tribal traditions. On "two-hearts" or witches, see also Simmons.

61. Murie (1981), pp. 173–175.

62. See Skinner, pp. 81–83, 182–183.

63. See Paul Coze, *L'Oiseau-Tourneau; paysages et magie peau-rouges* (Paris, 1938); see also William Tomkins, *Universal Sign Language of the Plains Indians* (San Diego, Calif.: 1926), p. 79.

64. See Ralph Buckstaff, "Stars and Constellations of a Pawnee Sky Map," in *American Anthropologist,* 29 (1927), pp. 279–285. The bundle is held at the University of Chicago.

65. See Edward Curtis, *The North American Indian,* vol. 19 (New York: 1930), p. 53.

66. See Arthur Versluis, *Song of the Cosmos: An Introduction to Traditional Cosmology* (Bridport, England: Prism, 1991) for a discussion of giants and of the Flood in different traditions.

67. See note 66 above.

68. George Bird Grinnell, *Blackfoot Lodge Tales: The Story of a Prairie People* (Lincoln, Neb.: University of Nebraska Press, 1962), p. 137.

69. Murie (1981), I.40, 139; II.433.

70. See Walker, pp. 78–79, 84–85, 154–155.

71. This is why it is said among many tribes that to take a scalp of an enemy means that he will accompany and serve the victor in the next world. The scalp, after all, comes from the crown of the head, the fontanel, "through which" the subtle modalities of the individual "pass." This is recognized in virtually all traditions; it is the implicit significance of water on the head in Christian baptism, which purifies the soul virtually. The spiritual significance for the afterlife of the crown of the head is recognized explicitly in Tibetan Buddhist and Taoist traditions, as well as in yogic Indian and Celtic traditions. The crown of the head is atop the subtle-body axis.

72. See Hultkranz (1987) on the divisions between the northern hunter and the

southern agrarian traditions. Often these were mixed, and one finds much evidence of a highly centralized community in the Midwest, not only at Cahokia but in Ohio and even in Michigan, as we will discuss shortly in regard to agriculture.

73. Brown, ed., p. 7.

74. See Henry Corbin, *Spiritual Body and Celestial Earth* (Princeton, N.J.: Bollingen, 1977), pp. 160–161.

75. Corbin, p. 71.

76. See William Bartram, *The Travels of William Bartram* (New York: Macy, 1928), pp. 359–361. See also Lucius Apuleius, *The Golden Ass,* and the Isaic initiatory symbolism.

77. See Arthur Versluis, *The Egyptian Mysteries* (London: Penguin, 1988).

78. See Grinnell, vol. 2 (1962), pp. 293–327.

79. See Kohl, pp. 40–41, 150–154.

80. Kohl, pp. 152–153.

81. See Brown, ed., especially pp. 42ff.

82. Although baptism constitutes an initiation, there nevertheless is no Christian initiatory transmission from *master to disciple* in the Sufi or Buddhist sense, save in Orthodoxy.

83. More than one Navaho has expressed frustration that white society does not regard as criminal what the tribes regard as the worst of all crimes—sorcerous ones.

84. See Selwyn Dewdney, *The Sacred Scrolls of the Southern Ojibway* (Toronto: University of Toronto Press, 1975), pp. 114ff.; see also William Warren, *History of the Ojibways* (1885; reprint; St. Paul, Minn.: Minnesota Historical Society Press, 1957), pp. 108–111; and Henry Schoolcraft, *Oneota; or, the Red Race of America* (New York: Wiley & Putnam, 1845), p. 454.

85. See Kluckhohn and also note 54 above.

86. See Curtis, "The Wichita," in *The North American Indian,* vol. 19, pp. 55ff.

87. See Thomas Mails, *Fool's Crow* (New York: Doubleday, 1979), pp. 162ff., for an account of contemporary medicine men among the Sioux.

88. See Guénon (1953); see too his *The Crisis of the Modern World* (London: Luzac, 1975). One might also look at the works of A. K. Coomaraswamy, particularly essays like those in *The Bugbear of Literacy,* to see the antitraditional action of the modern world in India. The same destruction of traditional culture Coomaraswamy discusses in Asia happened also in America and continues to the present day. The principles of tradition, and of its destruction, remain everywhere the same.

89. See in this regard Martin Lings, *The Eleventh Hour* (Oxford: Quinta Essentia, 1988).

90. See James Barr, "Of Metaphysics and Polynesian Navigation," in *Avaloka: A Journal of Traditional Religion and Culture,* 4 (1989).

91. Compare Weltfish, pp. 250–251.

92. See A. K. Coomaraswamy, *Yaksas* (New Delhi: Munshiram, 1980).

93. This is not to discount the seafaring peoples; we are speaking here only of the landlubbers.

94. See Weltfish, pp. 210ff., 238ff.

95. Chief John Snow, *These Mountains Are Our Sacred Places* (Toronto: Stevens, 1977), p. 145.

96. Sadruddin Muhammad Shirazi, *Kitab al-hikmat al'arshiya* (Book of the Theosophy of the Throne), quoted in Corbin, p. 165.

97. See John Napoleon Brinton Hewitt, *Iroquoian Cosmology. Twenty-first Annual Report of the Bureau of American Ethnology*, 1903, pp. 127–339; *Forty-third Annual Report of the Bureau of American Ethnology*, 1928, pp. 449–819.

98. This description corresponds to certain Tibetan Buddhist traditions regarding "earlier" or "higher" states of human existence not bound by corporeality. It is not that these divine states no longer exist; it is that we are exiled from them into corporeality, which is at once a curse and a gift.

99. See James Cowan, *Mysteries of the Dream-Time* (Bridport, England: Prism, 1990), for a discussion of nomadic spiritual traditions.

100. Matthew 6:19–20.

101. See George Bird Grinnell, *Pawnee Hero Stories and Folk Tales* (Lincoln, Nebr.: University of Nebraska Press, 1961), p. 359.

102. See René Guénon, *The Symbolism of the Cross,* rev. ed., translated by A. Macnab (London: Luzac, 1975). Tribal peoples can appear to accept the Christian tradition outwardly but maintain their own traditions inwardly: the form often appears to be the same, but the meaning is radically different. This apparent assimilationism has appeared across all the Americas; it is one way the Amerindian religions have survived under extreme oppression. The difference between the Native American and the Christian cross symbolizes this situation.

103. Alternatively, the north may be black, and the west may be white. Traditional symbolism is not bound to be uniform, for what matters are not the symbols but that which they represent. Black and white can each signify transcendence, or purification, and indeed, can be transposed depending upon what is being signified. This transposability amounts, in the "Contrary" tradition of the Prairie tribes, to a kind of law, and corresponds to the widespread recognition that in Paradise a kind of "reversal" of terrestrial laws holds true.

104. See Neihardt, ed., pp. 32–33; see also Brown, ed., p. 7.

105. Brown, ed., p. 7.

106. On the symbolism of the north see Versluis (1991).

107. On this prohibition as noted among the Creeks, see Ruth Benedict, *The Concept of the Guardian Spirit in North America. Memoirs of the American Anthropological Association*, 29 (1923), p. 79; see also Benjamin Hawkins, *The Creek Confederacy. Collections of the Georgia Historical Society,* vol. 3 (Savannah, Georgia, 1848), p. 78.

108. Brown, ed., pp. 127ff.

109. See Adrian Snodgrass, *The Symbolism of the Stupa* (Ithaca, N.Y.: Cornell University Press, 1985).

110. See René Guénon, "The Meaning of the Octagon," translated by Alvin Moore, in *Avaloka: A Journal of Traditional Religion and Culture,* 6, no. 1 (1990–

1991). See also Guénon, *Fundamental Symbols of Sacred Science* (Cambridge: Quinta Essentia, forthcoming).

111. See W. Y. Evans-Wentz, *Cuchama and Sacred Mountains* (Chicago : Swallow Press, 1981), pp. 39–41.

112. See Murie, vol. 1 (1981), p. 79; see also the *Twenty-second Annual Report of the Bureau of American Ethnology,* vol. 2 (1904), p. 233.

113. On the *kalamakara,* see Snodgrass, pp. 312ff.

114. See St. Dionysius the Areopagite, *The Celestial Hierarchy.*

115. See Schuon (1990), pp. 74, 53, 56.

116. There is a similar symbolism entailed in the Hindu symbolism of Kali and Shiva, both of whom are Destroyers and yet are Divine. One thinks too of the Judeo-Christian precept "fear of the Lord is the beginning of wisdom" and of Jakob Böhme's assertion that "every created intellectual Being remaineth in its deeds and essences . . . and therein it beholdeth and feeleth God, as who is everywhere, whether it be in the Love or in the Wrath. . . . All places are alike to it, if it be in God's Love; and if it be not there, every place is Hell alike," in *Dialogues on the Supersensual Life,* translated by W. Law, vol. 3 (New York: Ungar, n.d.), p. 93.

117. Ake Hultkranz, *The Religions of the American Indians* (Berkeley, Calif.: University of California Press, 1979) p. 63.

118. Hultkranz (1979), p. 61.

119. Big White Owl [Jasper Hill], "Let Us Save America," in *Indians at Work* (Washington, D.C.: U.S. Department of the Interior, Office of Indian Affairs, January 1941), pp. 30–31.

120. Neihardt, ed., p. 232.

121. See W. H. Prescott, *History of the Conquest of Mexico and History of the Conquest of Peru* (New York: Random House, 1847), pp. 343ff., 1121ff.

122. Joel 2:28.

123. See Johannes Tauler, *Sermons* (New York: Paulist Press, 1985), pp. 146–147, sermon 44.

124. See note 123 above.

125. See, on the three parts of the being and on spiritual power, Arthur Amiotte, "The Lakota Sun Dance," in DeMallie and Parks, eds., pp. 87–88.

126. Sherrard (1987), p. 46.

127. See Walker, pp. 113–114.

128. For an indication of the ways dreams and visions have appeared in Judeo-Christian tradition see Daniel 2, for Daniel's interpretation of the dream of Nebuchadnezzar. This dream had clear cosmological significance and referred directly to the four ages of humanity—golden, silver, brass, and iron—found also in other traditions. In Judeo-Christian, in Muslim, in Buddhist, and in Hindu traditions essentially the same spiritual truths are found and, to a considerable extent, similar means of spiritual revelation, renewal, and practice.

129. Schuon (1990), pp. 77–78.

130. Schuon (1990), p. 79.

131. See René Guénon, "Silence and Solitude," translated by Peter Hickey in *Avaloka: A Journal of Traditional Religion and Culture,* (forthcoming).

132. Brown, ed., p. 60.

133. Brown, ed., p. 58.

134. Neihardt, ed., p. 36.

135. The spotted eagle symbolizes the intellect, in Hindu tradition called *buddhi.* See Brown, ed., p. 6.

136. Brown, ed., p. 41.

137. *Topeka Capital-Journal,* 27 April 1991, p. 1. Italics added.

138. Bartram, p. 386.

BIBLIOGRAPHY

'Abd Al-Karim Al-Jili. *Universal Man.* Translated by Titus Burckhardt. Sherborne, England: Beshara, 1983.

Barr, James. "Of Metaphysics and Polynesian Navigation." In *Avaloka: A Journal of Traditional Religion and Culture,* 4 (1989): 1–3ff.

Bartram, William. *The Travels of William Bartram.* New York: Macy, 1928.

Benedict, Ruth. *The Concept of the Guardian Spirit in North America. Memoirs of the American Anthropological Association,* 29 (1923).

Boas, Franz. *The Religion of the Kwakiutl Indians.* New York: Columbia University Press, 1930.

Bowers, Alfred W. *Mandan Social and Ceremonial Organization.* Chicago: University of Chicago Press, 1950.

Brown, Joseph Epes, ed. *The Sacred Pipe.* New York: Penguin, 1972.

Buckstaff, Ralph. "Stars and Constellations of a Pawnee Sky Map." In *American Anthropologist,* 29 (1927): 279–285.

Catlin, George. *Letters and Notes on the Manners, Customs, and Conditions of North American Indians.* 2 vols. 1844. Reprint. New York: Dover, 1973.

Clifford, Terry. *Tibetan Buddhist Medicine.* New York: Weiser, 1986.

Collier, John. *The Indians of the Americas.* New York: Norton, 1947.

Coomaraswamy, A. K. *The Vedas.* Beckenham, England: Prologos, 1976.

———. *Yaksas.* New Delhi: Munshiram, 1980.

Corbin, Henry. *Spiritual Body and Celestial Earth.* Princeton, N.J.: Bollingen, 1977.

Cowan, James. *Mysteries of the Dream-Time.* Bridport, England: Prism, 1990.

Curtis, Edward S. *The North American Indian.* 20 vols. New York: 1930.

DeMallie, R. J., and D. R. Parks, eds. *Sioux Indian Religion.* Norman, Okla.: University of Oklahoma Press, 1987.

Densmore, Frances. *Teton Sioux Music. Smithsonian Bulletin,* 61 (1918).

Dewdney, Selwyn. *The Sacred Scrolls of the Southern Ojibway.* Toronto: University of Toronto Press, 1975.

Dugan, Kathleen Margaret. *The Vision Quest of the Plains Indians: Its Spiritual Significance.* Lampeter, Wales: Edwin Mellen Press, 1985.

Eastman, Charles (Ohiyesa). *The Soul of the Indian.* Boston: Houghton, 1911.

Evans-Wentz, W. Y. *Cuchama and Sacred Mountains.* Chicago: Swallow Press, 1981.

Grinnell, George Bird. *Pawnee Hero Stories and Folk Tales.* Lincoln, Nebr.: University of Nebraska Press, 1961.

———. *The Cheyenne Indians: Their History and Ways of Life.* New York: Cooper, 1962.

Guénon, René. *The Reign of Quantity and the Signs of the Times.* London: Luzac, 1953.

———. *The Crisis of the Modern World.* London: Luzac, 1975.

———. *The Symbolism of the Cross.* Rev. ed. Translated by A. Macnab. London: Luzac, 1975.

———. "The Meaning of the Octagon." Translated by Alvin Moore. In *Avaloka: A Journal of Traditional Religion and Culture,* 6, no.1 (1990–1991): 33–37.

Harrod, Howard. *Renewing the World: Plains Indian Religion and Morality.* Tucson: University of Arizona Press, 1987.

Hawkins, Benjamin. *The Creek Confederacy. Collections of the Georgia Historical Society.* Savannah, Georgia, 1848.

Herrera, Antonio de. *General History of the Continent and Islands of America.* Translated by Capt. John Stevens. London: 1726.

Hewitt, John Napoleon Brinton. *Iroquoian Cosmology. Twenty-first Annual Report of the Bureau of American Ethnology,* 1903: 127–339; *Forty-third Annual Report of the Bureau of American Ethnology,* 1928: 449–819.

Hultkranz, Ake. *The Religions of the American Indians.* Berkeley, Calif.: University of California Press, 1979.

———. *Belief and Worship in Native North America.* Syracuse, N.Y.: Syracuse University Press, 1981.

———. *Native Religions of North America.* New York: Harper & Row, 1987.

Kluckhohn, Clyde. *Navaho Witchcraft.* Boston: Beacon Press, 1944.

Kohl, Johann Georg. *Kitchi-Gami: Life Among the Lake Superior Ojibway.* Translated by L. Wraxall. 1860. Reprint. St. Paul, Minn.: Minnesota Historical Society Press, 1985.

Lings, Martin. *The Eleventh Hour.* Oxford: Quinta Essentia, 1988.

————. *Symbol and Archetype*. Oxford: Quinta Essentia, 1991.

Lowers, Alfred. *Mandan Social and Ceremonial Organization*. Chicago: University of Chicago Press, 1950.

Lowie, Robert. "Arikara Societies." In *Anthropological Papers of the American Museum of Natural History*, 11 (1915): 674–675.

Mails, Thomas. *Fool's Crow With Frank Fool's Crow*. New York: Doubleday, 1979.

Mallam, Clark. *Site of the Serpent: A Prehistoric Life Metaphor in South Central Kansas*. Lyons, Kansas: Coronado-Quivira Museum, No. 1, n.d.

Müller, Werner. *Pre-Columbian American Religions*. Translated by S. Davis. London: Weidenfeld, 1968.

Murie, James. "Pawnee Societies." In *Anthropological Papers of the American Museum of Natural History*, 11 (1915): 580–581.

————. *Ceremonies of the Pawnee*. 2 vols. Washington, D.C.: Smithsonian Inst., 1981.

Nasr, Seyyed Hossein. *Man and Nature: The Spiritual Crisis of Modern Man*. Kuala Lumpur, Malaysia: Foundation for Traditional Studies, 1976.

————. *Knowledge and the Sacred*. New York: Crossroad, 1981.

Neihardt, John C., ed. *Black Elk Speaks*. 1932. Reprint. New York: Pocket, 1972.

Prescott, W. H. *History of the Conquest of Mexico and History of the Conquest of Peru*. New York: Random House, 1847.

Radin, Paul, ed. *Crashing Thunder: The Autobiography of an American Indian*. New York: Appleton, 1926.

————. *The Road of Life and Death*. New York: Pantheon, 1945.

Schaya, Leo. *The Universal Meaning of the Kabbala*. London: Allen and Unwin, 1973.

Scholem, Gerschom. *Kabbalah*. Jerusalem: Keter, 1974.

Schoolcraft, Henry. *Oneota; or, the Red Race of America*. New York: Wiley & Putnam, 1845.

————. *Notes on the Iroquois*. New York: Bartlett, 1846.

————. *History of the Indian Tribes of the United States*. Philadelphia: Lippincott, 1854.

Schuon, Frithjof. *Light on the Ancient Worlds*. Bloomington, Ind.: World Wisdom, 1984.

————. *The Feathered Sun: Plains Indians in Art and Philosophy*. Bloomington: World Wisdom, 1990.

Sherrard, Philip. *The Eclipse of Man and Nature*. London: Golgonooza, 1987.

————. *The Sacred in Life and Art*. London: Golgonooza, 1990.

Simmons, Leo, ed. *Sun Chief: The Autobiography of a Hopi Indian*. New Haven, Conn.: Yale University Press, 1970.

Skinner, Alanson. "Social Life and Ceremonial Bundles of the Menominee Indians." In *Anthropological Papers of the American Museum of Natural History*, no. 1 (1913): 1–557.

Snodgrass, Adrian. *The Symbolism of the Stupa*. Ithaca, N.Y.: Cornell University Press, 1985.

Snow, Chief John. *These Mountains Are Our Sacred Places.* Toronto: Stevens, 1977.

Southcott, Mary E. *The Sound of the Drum: The Sacred Art of the Anishnabec.* Erin, Ontario: Boston Mills Press, 1984.

Speck, Frank. *A Study of the Delaware Indian Big House Ceremony.* Publication of the Pennsylvania Historical Commission, 1931.

Squier, E.G. *The Serpent Symbol and the Worship of the Reciprocal Principles of Nature in America.* New York: Putnam, 1851.

———. *Antiquities of the State of New York.* Buffalo, N.Y.: Derby, 1851.

Tauler, Johannes. *Sermons.* New York: Paulist Press, 1985.

Tedlock, Dennis, and Barbara Tedlock, eds. *Teachings from the American Earth.* New York: Liveright, 1975.

Tomkins, William. *Universal Sign Language of the Plains Indians.* San Diego, Calif.: 1926.

Tooker, Elizabeth, ed. *Native North American Spirituality of the Eastern Woodlands.* New York: Paulist Press, 1979.

Versluis, Arthur. "In the Tracks of the Buddha: The Footprint Image and Its Meanings." In *Avaloka: A Journal of Traditional Religion and Culture,* 1, no. 2 (1987) 17ff.

———. *The Egyptian Mysteries.* London: Penguin, 1988.

———. *Song of the Cosmos: An Introduction to Traditional Cosmology.* Bridport, England: Prism, 1991.

Walker, James R. *Lakota Ritual and Belief.* Lincoln, Nebr.: University of Nebraska Press, 1980.

Warren, William. *History of the Ojibways.* 1885. Reprint. St. Paul, Minn.: Minnesota Historical Society Press, 1957.

Waters, Frank. *Book of the Hopi.* 1963. Reprint. New York: Penguin, 1982.

Wedel, Waldo. *Prehistoric Man on the Great Plains.* Norman, Okla.: University of Oklahoma Press, 1961.

Weltfish, Gene. *The Lost Universe: Pawnee Life and Culture.* Lincoln, Neb.: University of Nebraska Press, 1965.

Wissler, Clark. *The Relation of Nature to Man in Aboriginal America.* New York: Oxford University Press, 1926.

Index

VOICES OF THE FIRST DAY

AWAKENING IN THE ABORIGINAL DREAMTIME

Robert Lawlor
0-89281-320-2 • $24.95 pb
More than 150 color, duotone, and black and white images,
including bark paintings, drawings, photographs, and engravings from
the early twentieth century, many never before published

". . . a remarkably comprehensive and fascinating account of the Aboriginal world view and its potential usefulness in imagining future directions for our own faltering culture. Lawlor's careful, accessible exploration of Aboriginal customs and beliefs, plus a spectacular collection of art, are truly worthwhile." **Kirkus Reviews**

". . . vital, vibrant . . . a careful examination—in full anthropological detail—of how the primal Australian cultures saw the world and a primer for our learning once more to see it in that necessary way, before it is too late, before all the primal guides have gone."
Kirkpatrick Sale, Author of *The Conquest of Paradise*

"The words and ideas breathe with a sense of our source; Mother-land and Dreaming Law." **Bobby McLeod**, Aboriginal poet, singer, and activist

A portion of the proceeds from the sale of this book go to the Denooch Aboriginal Healing Centre, which assists Aborigines free themselves from alcohol, drug, and tobacco addiction by employing tribal healing methods; and to the South Australian Earth Sanctuaries, which provide a home for Australia's endangered species.

Ring of Fire

An Indonesian Odyssey

Lawrence Blair, with Lorne Blair
0-89281-430-6 • $24.95 pb
More than 100 color and black and white photographs

The true story behind the internationally award-winning PBS television series, **Ring of Fire** charts the Blair brothers' ten-year journey through the world's largest and least-known archipelago—the islands of Indonesia. Amid seemingly impenetrable rainforests, erupting volcanoes, and unimaginable natural beauty, the brothers captured on film and in words the customs, beliefs, and wisdom of the islands' inhabitants.

Their odyssey began with a 2500–mile voyage through the Spice Islands, guided by the notorious Bugi pirates. An entire decade of exploration followed, during which the authors lived among cannibals in West New Guinea and the healers of Bali; encountered the man-eating dragons of Komodo and the elusive "dream wanderers" of Borneo. With extraordinary courage, humor, and passion for the unknown, they tell of one of the most intriguing journeys ever made, which will stand as an enduring record of a vanishing world.

"Incomparable adventure teeming with thrills, chills, mystery, and the bizarre." **Los Angeles Times**

"Sets sails and sights for lands as unfamiliar and spectacular as anything dreamed up for a Steven Spielberg movie. Thoroughly fascinating nearly every harrowing step of the way." **Washington Post**

MANITOU

THE SACRED LANDSCAPE of NEW ENGLAND's NATIVE CIVILIZATION

James W. Mavor, Jr. and Byron E. Dix
0-89281-078-5 • $18.95 pb
150 Illustrations

In the summer of 1974 in the green hills of Vermont, Byron Dix discovered the first of at least twenty-five areas in New England believed to be ancient Native American ritual sites. Dix and coauthor James Mavor tell the fascinating story of the discovery and exploration of these many stone structures and standing stones, whose placement in the surrounding landscape suggests that they played an important role in celestial observation and shamanic ritual.

". . . among the few innovative advances in the field of New England archaeology in recent years . . . looks at a class of data which are ordinarily overlooked by both prehistorians and historians, and begins to fit them into a new paradigm . . . sensitively written and generally well-supported by documentary and excavational evidence."

Massachusetts Archaeological Society

"Manitou's ground-breaking treatment, handsomely illustrated with photos, maps, and line drawings, will unquestionably propel the emerging field of American geomancy considerably forward. A contemplation of the manitou worldview, presented here with excellence and mature excitement, yields a radically different appraisal of a fundamental aspect of our national history and geography, while suggesting new land–use and conservation parameters for the future." *Yoga Journal*

Navajo and Tibetan Sacred Wisdom

The Circle of the Spirit

Peter Gold • 0-89281-411-X • $29.95 pb
175 color and black-and-white illustrations

The similarity between Navajos and Tibetans has often been noted by scholars: the mandala sand paintings common to both cultures, their profound ideas about matter and spirit, as well as the uncanny physical resemblance between the two peoples. In *Navajo and Tibetan Sacred Wisdom*, anthropologist Peter Gold draws extensive parallels between the two cultures' creation myths, cosmology, geomancy, psychology, visionary arts, and healing and initiation rituals.

"A bold and exciting exploration, showing many astonishing parallels between these precious and imperiled traditions, from which our own world-weary western culture has so much to learn." **Peter Matthiessen**
Author of *The Snow Leopard* and *Indian Country*

"At long last the mighty indigenous traditions of Navajo and Tibetan are juxtaposed, to let their powerful teachings reinforce each other and resound together. A beautiful, wise book." **Joanna Macy**
Author of *World as Lover, World as Self*

These and other Inner Traditions titles are available at many fine bookstores or, to order directly from the publisher, send a check or money order for the total amount, payable to Inner Traditions, plus $3.00 shipping and handling for the first book and $1.00 for each additional book to:

Inner Traditions
One Park Street
Rochester, VT 05767

Be sure to request a free catalog.